# OUR GREAT GOD

## 24 Weekly Bible Lessons for Adults

### TEACH ME YOUR PATHS BOOK FIVE

TEACH ME YOUR PATHS
BOOK FIVE

# OUR GREAT GOD

## 24 Weekly Bible Lessons for Adults

# Gary S. Maxey

**WATS Publications**

ISBN: 9798670700825

**Published by**

**WATS Publications**
West Africa Theological Seminary
36 Olukunle Akinola Street
Ipaja, Lagos, NIGERIA

**Contact Addresses:**
Gary S. Maxey, Founder, WATS, PMB 003, Ipaja, Lagos
**Email:** drgarymaxey@gmail.com; Tel: +234-808-726-6310
To order copies, please contact: sales@watspublications.com
Tel: +234 (0) 803 781 2817; 806 875 2197


Designed and printed by
asbot**graphics**

# Table of Contents

Contents

# OTHER BOOKS BY GARY S. MAXEY

The WATS Journey: A Personal Narrative

New Life in Christ

Capturing a Lost Vision:
Can Nigeria's Greatest Revival Live Again?

The Seduction of the Nigerian Church

Discovering the New Testament

Discovering the Old Testament

Confessions of a Grateful Pilgrim

The Highway of Holiness

Standing Firm in Christ

The Thessalonian Road:
Sanctification Made Plain

Living Nigeria on Purpose, Vol. 1  4

Juju vs. Christianity: An African Dilemma

Igbé Ayé Titun Nínú Kristì *(New Life in Christ, Yoruba)*

# FOREWORD

There is no continent in the world where belief in a powerful Creator God is more firmly held than Africa. Atheism is virtually unheard of in Africa. This age-old belief is one of the reasons (though not the only one) why Africa is also the only continent in the history of the world to become majority Christian in a single century. Systematic theologies written in the Western world sometimes consume a huge amount of space for multiple "proofs" for the existence of God, but no such ink and paper are required in Africa.

Even more so than within African Traditional Religion, however, Christianity is a thoroughly God-centered faith. While Africans have agreed for centuries that the Creator God truly exists, the primary attention within their belief systems is elsewhere. Ultimately, they focus on people, as well as on the struggle of human beings with the invisible spirit world. Not so with the Bible, however. There the primary focus is on God.

Our faith is God-centered, or theocentric. That is why it is important in this book for us to explore what the Bible tells us about our great God. Who is this wonderful God who created the heavens and the earth, and who eventually created humans as male and female? How can we describe this God?

*Teach Me Your Paths* is a series of books designed to help us become better disciples of Jesus Christ. We seek to explore all aspects of our Christian faith, and especially to understand the Holy Bible as the core of God's revelation to humankind. We also want to learn to obey or observe everything Jesus has commanded. We take our cue from the psalmist, who cried to God to teach him his paths. *"Show me Your ways, O LORD; Teach me your paths"* (Psalm 25:4 NKJV; see also Psalm 86:11).

This is the fifth in a series of twelve volumes covering the broad scope of Christian doctrine. We started with *New Life in Christ*. If you have not studied that book I strongly urge you to get it and go through it. New life in Christ is the very essential starting point for our exploration of the Christian faith. Having experienced that starting point, we then turned in this series to the doctrinal foundation of our faith — the Bible, which is the holy word of God.

God gave us the Bible with both an Old Testament and a New Testament. Neither of them is intended to stand on its own. The Bible is incomplete without the Old Testament and it is equally incomplete without the New Testament. People who purchase and carry around a New Testament without the Old Testament must understand that they are carrying only one part of the written word of God.

*Exploring the Old Testament* is the second book in this series. Without the Old Testament we would not have clear ideas about how the world around us was created, how man was created, how sin entered into the world, and why the coming of a Messiah was so important. Our understanding of the nature of God himself would be much weaker. We would not have the incredibly powerful testimonies of God's dealings with Israel over a long history. We would not have the powerful worship guidance found in the Book of Psalms and other places. In discovering these and many other themes and truths we will see that the Old Testament provides us with foundations for our faith that are exceedingly important and without which we would be highly impoverished.

*Exploring the New Testament* is the third book. There we took time to understand the world of the New Testament, including the geographical, political and religious background to the life and times of Jesus and the first apostles. We then explored the twenty-seven books of the New Testament, in an effort to see why the life, death and resurrection of Jesus was so important and who and how the Christian Church emerged in the First Century.

The fourth book in this series is *Standing Firm in Christ*. In that book we took up where we left off in the first book, dealing with our personal spiritual life made possible through Jesus Christ. We discovered in some detail how important it is for all of us to not only be born again but to mature in a life of obedience to God and rich service to others.

In this book, *Our Great God*, we are moving to what we sometimes call theology proper, which is the study of God. Our study is divided into five parts. In Part One (Lessons 1-7) we introduce the study of God by exploring the various ways in which God is understood in our world. God is truly there, as we know, but he is perceived differently from one culture to another. We will also then take a look at the fundamental nature of God as trinity. Trinity is one of the most difficult aspects of God for our small human brains, yet it is definitely revealed in scripture. God is one, but he is also three.

Part Two (Lessons 8-11) introduces us to an understanding of God the Father. We know him as the First Person of the trinity. We will explore what the Bible teaches about God the Father as Creator and what we learn about him from both the Old Testament and the New Testament.

Part Three (Lessons 12-18) gives us the Bible teaching about God the Son, the Second Person of the trinity. Because Jesus Christ, the Son of God, was incarnated into human flesh and lived and died on earth, we know much more about him than we do about God the Father and God the Holy Spirit. We see him revealed in the Old Testament in various ways, including the forward-looking messianic prophecies of men such as Isaiah, Micah and Zechariah. We will take time to explore the miracle of his virgin birth, his earthly ministry, and his passion, death and resurrection. We will also note the ongoing ministry of

Jesus Christ and his anticipated Second Coming.

In Part Four (Lessons 19  24), we will study the person and ministry of God the Holy Spirit. We will see great lessons about the Holy Spirit in both the Old and New Testaments. We will focus attention on the ministry of the Holy Spirit at the birthplace of the Christian Church at Pentecost, as well as his ongoing ministry in the Church through the centuries.

This series started as a team effort many years ago. *New Life in Christ* was originally written by myself and several of my students, though it was later re-edited in its current format by myself.  All of the other volumes have been my sole responsibility. I accept full responsibility for any inaccuracies or inadequacies herein. The reader will note that in this book scripture references are quoted in the *New King James Version (NKJV)*. I might have preferred the *New English Translation* (NET), but I have chosen the NKJV because I know many of my readers still use the KJV with which they were first introduced to the Bible.

May you read and study with a God-fearing attitude!  If the study of this book helps you spiritually, I would be happy to know about it, and would also encourage you to study additional books that are forthcoming in the series.

August 2019
Rev. Dr. Gary S. Maxey, Founder
West Africa Theological Seminary

OUR GREAT GOD

# How to Use This Book

Our *Great God* may be used in a variety of ways, but it was primarily designed for use in a catechism class. Regularity of study is necessary for effective indoctrination. Therefore, the lessons should be studied one after the other on a weekly basis. Suitable venues for such study could include a Sunday school classes or, more ideally, weekday small groups designed specifically for discipleship.

It is important that students get and study their own lesson books. Lessons should be studied in advance. Weekly class should be conducted by a mature Christian worker or pastor and should be done in a lively manner. The suggested lesson format is a ninety-minute session divided as follows: ten minutes for opening activities (prayer, choruses); sixty minutes to cover one lesson; fifteen or twenty minutes for questions and answers. The presentation of the lesson should not be a mere lecture, but a creative presentation in which the group leader mixes in interactive questions and illustrations with the printed lesson contents. The students should be encouraged to participate actively in the discussion and take notes.

Experience has shown that under normal circumstances the class size should not be more than fifteen to twenty students, to more easily allow for interaction and class participation. In large churches the classes can be arranged into many groups, based on age, sex, native language or spiritual maturity.

Learning the Bible and studying doctrine should never be a boring or tiring matter. Therefore, encourage participation and liveliness in the classes on the part of both teachers and students. And, just as the students and group leaders make advance preparation before beginning the lesson study together, so it is advisable that the participants write out the answers to the questions for each lesson after they have studied in the class together. Depending on the circumstances it may be helpful for participants to write out answers after each lesson and submit them to the group leader in time for correction or comments before the next class session. In this manner, steady progress will be made, and learning will go on throughout several days each week.

God bless you as you study to show yourself approved unto Him!

# PART ONE

○○○○

# WHO IS OUR GOD?

People who talk about God can be divided into three groups: theists, atheists and agnostics. The first group, theists, accepts the idea that God exists, independent of human thought or existence. The second group, atheists, maintains that God does not exist, and is therefore a product of human imagination. The third group, agnostics, leaves the question of God's existence unanswered, maintaining that no one can know the truth about it. For them God may or may not exist.

Christians are theists, by definition. They believe that God exists. They further believe in Jesus Christ as the Son of God, which is why we are called Christians. The Bible is a theocentric, or God-centered book. It begins with God and ends with God. The first book of the Bible, Genesis, begins with the words, "In the beginning God . . ." (Gen. 1:1). The last book of the Bible, Revelation, ends with the words, "The grace of our Lord Jesus Christ be with you all. Amen" (Rev. 22:21). There is only one book in the Bible where the name of God is not mentioned (the Book of Esther), though even in that book the action and presence of God can be seen between the lines. In most of the books of the Bible the presence, or action, or words of God are present from beginning to end. That is why first and foremost we take the Bible as a revelation from God and about God.

In this book our study is to discover as much as we can about our great God. Who is he? How can we describe him? What do we know about his character? How can we describe his actions? What can we say about his personality?

One of the greatest mysteries about our great God is the reality of the trinity. The word "trinity" is not found in the Bible. It was coined around 200 years after the birth of Christ. Tertullian, an African living in the Carthage, in modern-day Tunisia, was the first Christian to use the term "trinity." However, even though "trinity" is not found in the Bible it is an acceptable word to describe the mysterious fact that our great God is both one but also somehow three. It is a mystery that defies full human understanding.

Indeed, one of the lessons we learn early on in the scriptures is that while our great God is quite real he is of such a nature that he cannot be fully comprehended by humans. The reason is not difficult to grasp. We humans are finite, and exceedingly limited in our understanding. Who among us can understand the vastness of the universe on a starry night? Who can explain the mystery of life within the sub-microscopic world? How much more, then, can we expect to understand an infinite and glorious God who created it all? That is why we say, "A God comprehended is no God at all!" The lesser can never understand the greater. As wonderful and marvelous as the tiny ants are, they cannot begin to fathom how you are able to read this book.

There is an interesting story in the Book of Exodus about one man's quest to know God better. Moses first encountered God at a burning bush that was not consumed by the flames. There he spoke with a mysterious God whose name, he was told, was Yahweh. Eventually Moses knew more about God, yet he was never satisfied. Deuteronomy 34:10 says, "there has not arisen in Israel a prophet like Moses, whom the Lord knew face to face." Yet even Moses found out, as we can see in Exodus 33, that he could never know God fully.

In this first part of our study we will ask some of the most basic questions about our great God. In the subsequent parts we will look at each person within the trinity: God the Father, God the Son, and God the Holy Spirit. As we go through these studies we pray that each of us will get to know our great God better, and that we will determine, as Joshua said about himself and his family: "As for me and my house, we will serve the Lord" (Joshua 24:15).

# IS GOD TRULY THERE?

Psalm 19:1; 1 Timothy 6:15-16; Hebrews 11:1-2

*The heavens declare the glory of God; and the firmament[a] shows His handiwork. . . . He who is the blessed and only Potentate, the King of kings and Lord of lords, who alone has immortality, dwelling in unapproachable light, whom no man has seen or can see, to whom be honor and everlasting power. Amen. . . . God, who at various times and in various ways spoke in time past to the fathers by the prophets, has in these last days spoken to us by His Son, whom He has appointed heir of all things, through whom also He made the worlds;*

## Lesson Theme

A strong belief in God is a sure foundation on which we stand as Christian believers. There are evidences of God all around us, and most especially within the Bible, which is God's revealed word to us. Yet even without the Bible we can learn that God exists and to a limited degree we can know something about him. Natural Theology is the study of what we can learn about God from nature, i.e., by observing the world around us. It is clear from an examination of our world that there is a benevolent, powerful and super intelligent Being behind it all. What we see in our world could never have happened without an Intelligent Designer. The very existence of our planet Earth, with all the finely-balanced elements that make human life possible, is a miracle. It could never have come to be merely by chance. For there to be such an awesome miracle there had to be a great Designer of some kind. When we look into the vast reaches of the university with the most powerful telescopes available, we are lost in awe and wonder and can see that it is the work of a great God. On the other hand, when we peer into the most powerful microscopes and see incredibly complex universes of teeming life far too small for the naked eye to perceive we have the same reaction. Without even opening our Bibles we are left in awe and wonder and we know that there is a great God behind it all.

## Introduction

Unbelieving atheists have scoffed at the idea of God's existence for thousands of years. The Bible calls them fools. Adam and Eve knew very well that God exists, and so did Satan, when he said to Eve, "Has God indeed said . . . ?" (Gen. 3:1). In that sense Satan and his demons are "believers," though they are in wicked rebellion against God. They know God exists. James said, "Even the demons believe — and tremble!" (James 2:19). We can see why God has pronounced a clear verdict on atheism: "The fool has said in his heart, 'There is no God'" (Psalm 14:1; 53:1).

What we will see in this lesson is the truth of those ancient words. Yet at the same time it is good to understand how and why we know God exists. There are evidences of his work all around us, and when we open our Bibles we can find truths about him about which we can be certain. In this lesson we will survey some of those evidences and truth.

## Lesson

1. At the beginning of this lesson we mentioned the field of Natural Theology. Theology in its simplest form means "the study of God," or "the study of the things related to God." What we think about God or what we understand about God is our theology. Thus, everyone has his or her theology. But the most important question for us is whether or not our theology agrees with the revealed truth of God's word, since the Bible is the foundation of all knowledge. However, we can talk about Natural Theology as what we can learn about God not through the Bible but by observing the world around us. What can we learn about God by observing nature? Romans 1:20 says, "For since the creation of the world God's invisible qualities — his eternal power and divine nature — have been clearly seen, being understood from what has been made, so that people are without excuse."

**The Bible teaches us how to trust a God who is truly there but whom we cannot see with our human eyes.**

2.  What we are saying is that we know that God exists simply by observing his creation all around us. The Bible says that "In the beginning, God created the heavens and the earth" (Gen. 1:1), but even without the Bible in our hands we can know that our world had to be created by a wonderful and benevolent being. This is what Job says plainly in Job 12:7-10. "But ask the animals, and they will teach you, or the birds in the sky, and they will tell you; or speak to the earth, and it will teach you, or let the fish in the sea inform you. Which of all these does not know that the hand of the Lord has done this? In his hand is the life of every creature and the breath of all mankind." Only in recent years has science developed to the point of creating marvelous mechanical, electrical and digital inventions, yet none of man's inventions come anywhere close to the marvels of the created universe.

3.  When we turn to modern science and understand their uncovering of the marvels of our universe we see even greater reasons to know that God is behind it all. When we think about the marvel of human vision and the

human eye and begin to uncover some of its mysteries through modern science we know that there is a great God behind it. As we peer into the most powerful electron microscopes and see sub-atomic worlds moving in complex and precise order we know it can only be possible because of a great and awesome Creator. This is what prompted the psalmist to write, "For you created my inmost being; you knit me together in my mother's womb. I praise you because I am fearfully and wonderfully made; your works are wonderful, I know that full well" (Psalm 139:13-14).

4.  Modern science has enabled us to see that the planet Earth is sustained in a delicate balance that enables human life to survive and thrive. If the earth were closer to the sun, we could not survive. If the balance of gases in the air we breathe were different we could not survive. Everything had to be created by a God who knew exactly what was needed to sustain our lives and to enable us to go about our duties with assurance of safety and security. There are dozens of Bible assurances of the sustaining hand of God over his creation and over us as his children. Isaiah 41:10, for example, says "So do not fear, for I am with you; do not be dismayed, for I am your God. I will strengthen you and help you; I will uphold you with my righteous right hand."

5.  The strongest source of our confidence in the reality of God is through the Bible, the written revelation of God himself to humankind. It is from beginning to end a

revelation of God, telling us who he is, what he is like, what he has done, and how he seeks a relationship with men and women as his favored creation. Without the Bible we could know that God exists and that he created this world, but we would not know much at all about his character, about the story of his creation of the world, and about his marvelous plan of salvation for all of humanity. The Bible is definitely our bedrock foundation of understanding about God.

6. The reality and the existence of God is further evidenced by the thousands and even millions of testimonies of people down through the ages who have known God, who have talked with God, and who have left their personal testimonies about it. The Bible starts with the story of Adam and Eve and their encounter with and relationship with the Creator God. Virtually every book of the Bible contains evidences of God communicating with human beings. The stories of believers in the ages after the completion of the Bible are also powerful reminders that God is there because he communicates with men and women of every culture and every age.

7. The greatest personal revelation of God to men and women is through the miracle of salvation. People who are yet in their sins are walking in spiritual darkness, which means that their contact with God has been blocked. Isaiah expresses it this way: "Surely the arm of the Lord is not too short to save, nor his ear too dull to hear. But your iniquities have separated you from your God; your sins have hidden his face from you, so that

he will not hear" (Isaiah 59:1-2). With the miracle of salvation, the reality of God's existence and his presence becomes real to every believer.

8.  It is the miracle of communication with God that most powerfully persuades believers of the reality of the Creator God. How his presence is experienced by individual believers may vary from one person to another, but there is a universal conviction of the reality of God in the life of every true believer. Prayer is central to Christian existence and for a simple reason: it is our vital connection to the great God of the universe. Through prayer we not only can talk to God, but we can have the inner assurance that he is talking to us as well.

9.  The apostle Paul talks about the majesty of our God who dwells "in unapproachable light, whom no man has seen or can see" (1 Timothy 6:16). Jesus told the Samaritan woman at the well, "God is Spirit, and those who worship Him must worship in spirit and truth" (John 4:24). We cannot see God because he does not have a material body (though we also know that God the Son came to earth in a human form). This is why Colossians 1:15 refers to God as the "invisible God." Yet the great news is that because we have eternal salvation that has been purchased through the precious blood of Jesus we now have access to the heavenlies and to a never-ending assurance of the eternal reality of God. We can joyfully sing with the psalmist, "My soul longs, yes, even faints for the courts of the Lord; my

heart and my flesh cry out for the living God" (Psalm 84:2). Truly he is our great God!

## Questions

1.  What is Natural Theology, and what does it teach us about the reality of God?

2.  What does Job 12:7-10 tell us about the reality of God?

3.  How do telescopes and microscopes help us to know that there is a Creator God?

4.  What is our strongest source of confidence in the reality of God?

5.  How does the miracle of salvation convince us about the reality of God himself?

## Things to think about

❖ *Faith in the reality of a benevolent Creator God appears to be a fundamental part of what it means to be an African.*

❖ *Philosophical arguments for or against the existence of God have little meaning to one who has experienced personal salvation and who is in touch with God through daily prayer.*

# THE TRADITIONAL AFRICAN PERSPECTIVE

### Psalm 68:31; Isaiah 45:14

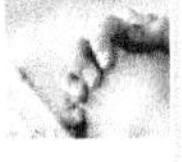

*Envoys will come from Egypt; Cush [i.e., the upper Nile region] will submit herself to God. . . . This is what the Lord says: "The products of Egypt and the merchandise of Cush, and those tall Sabeansthey will come over to you and will be yours; they will trudge behind you, coming over to you in chains. They will bow down before you and plead with you, saying, 'Surely God is with you, and there is no other; there is no other god.'"*

## Lesson Theme

We have seen that belief in the Creator God is quite strong in Africa. Atheism is virtually unknown. For long centuries Africans have believed in a single Creator God. This belief was there long before there were influences from Christianity, Judaism or Islam, which are regarded as the three great monotheistic world religions. In this lesson we will seek to understand how the Creator God has been understood within African societies over the centuries.

## Introduction

There are around two thousand distinct ethnic groups, or tribes, in Africa. Each of them has its own unique traditional belief system, or religion. However, there are so many elements in common between all of those belief systems that we can legitimately refer to African Traditional Religion as a whole. One area of common belief is that there is a single Creator God who was responsible for the creation of the world. Furthermore, there is a common conviction that this Creator God is powerful and benevolent. In this lesson we will understand more about how this Creator God is viewed among traditional Africans and how he relates to the created world and everything in it.

## Lesson

1. We start our look at the traditional African understanding of God by noting that the Bible makes many scores of references to Africa, though without using that exact word. There is disagreement about the origin of the word "Africa," though it was clearly in use at least shortly after Bible times. What we have in the Bible are references to numerous territories located on the African continent. Egypt, Ethiopia and Libya are the most common ones, and are mentioned numerous times. Generally speaking a distinction is made between Egypt, which was more ethnically akin to most of the inhabitants of Palestine, and Ethiopia, which referred to the darker skinned dwellers further south. For example, Jeremiah 13:23 raises the rhetorical question, "Can an

Ethiopian change his skin or a leopard its spots?" In the long table of nations in Genesis 10:6-20 there is a list of various kingdoms founded by the families of the founders of Ethiopia. Likewise, there are references to places such as Cush and Put (named after sons of Ham, Noah's second son, and ancestor of modern black Africans), which refer to territories in Africa. However, though Africa is thus referred to numerous times in the Bible we are left without answers about how the multiplied hundreds of tribes, especially in sub-Sahara Africa, eventually developed their distinctive religious systems.

**African Traditional Worldview**

**Creator God**          (creator/god)

**Spirit World**          lesser deities

nature spirits

Ancestral spirits

good/evil

impersonal spiritual power

**Physical World**

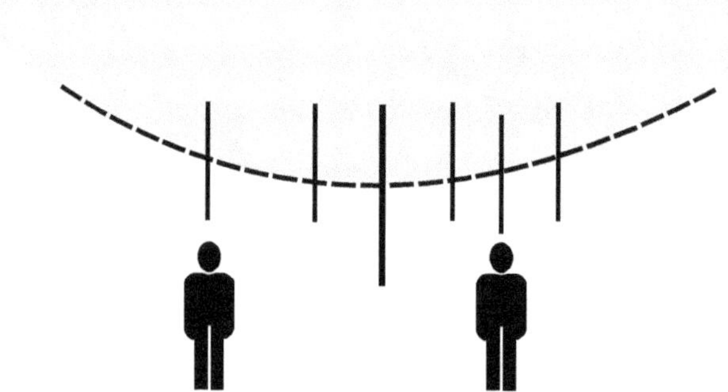

**The African worldview has similarities with the Bible worldview. However, it is more human-centered and less God-centered.**

2. We know from God's revelation in the Bible that all of humanity is descended from a common ancestry. We are all children of Adam and Eve. The story of the origins of humanity is clearly given in Genesis 1 3. We also know from Romans 1:18-32 that the truth of God that was revealed to our distant ancestors was eventually lost, as multitudes turned away from that truth. The descent into darkness that resulted is shared by cultures

all over the globe. In Romans 1:18-32 Paul explains that though all people once knew God many (even all, at one time or the other) fell away into darkness. Paul says, "For since the creation of the world His invisible *attributes* are clearly seen, being understood by the things that are made, *even* His eternal power and Godhead, so that they are without excuse, because, although they knew God, they did not glorify *Him* as God, nor were thankful, but became futile in their thoughts, and their foolish hearts were darkened" (vv. 20-21).

3. There are secular sociologists who do not accept the Bible truth that all nations around the world are descended from societies who once knew God's revelation. Therefore, they want us to believe that primitive human societies move from belief in many gods (polytheism) toward belief in one Creator God. They therefore have difficulty understanding why Africans for centuries were not polytheists, in the sense we see in Asia. Despite falling into darkness, we can see that Africans all over the continent retained truth about the reality of a single Creator God.

4. Within the African perspective a single Creator God is believed to be the ultimate source of the entire universe. He is further assumed to be both good and powerful. However, the common traditional African belief is that God is somehow hidden. The God who was once known and more visible is now withdrawn. There are many explanations. One Ghanaian tradition is that when God in ancient times peered down at an Ashanti woman pounding plantain with her pestle and mortar

the woman lifted the pestle too high and struck God in the nose, irritating him and causing him to withdraw. Whatever the cause may have been, God is now believed to be wholly transcendent. His immanence is only preserved in African names for God and proverbs, aphorisms, poetry, and pithy sayings associated with him.

5. As a result, direct worship of God within African traditional religion is rare. It is there to some extent among the Igbo of southeastern Nigeria and among the Ashanti of Ghana. However, almost always God is worshipped or accessed through intermediaries. For centuries Africans have focus their worship not on the infinite and remote Creator God but on idols representing intermediate deities or intermediaries. These intermediaries could be forces of nature (e.g., thunder), or natural objects such as rivers, forests or mountains. We know that the idolatry that accompanies such worship is thoroughly rejected in the Bible as one of the worst possible sins and offenses against God.

6. The Bible is clear about what it means to worship idols rather than God himself. Deuteronomy 32:16-17 says, "They provoked Him to jealousy with foreign *gods;* with abominations they provoked Him to anger. They sacrificed to demons, not to God, *to gods* they did not know, to new *gods,* new arrivals that your fathers did not fear." Paul, writing centuries later, said, "Rather, that the things which the Gentiles sacrifice they sacrifice to demons and not to God, and I do not want you to have fellowship with demons. You cannot drink the cup of

the Lord and the cup of demons; you cannot partake of the Lord's table and of the table of demons. Or do we provoke the Lord to jealousy? Are we stronger than He?" (1 Corinthians 10:20-22).

7.  The question that scholars have raised in recent years is whether traditional Africans are truly monotheists, or whether they are polytheists. While it is true that Africans traditionally believe in a single Creator God we can see that most of them also have revered and worshipped lesser deities. There are over 200 gods among traditional Yoruba worshippers, for example. While some scholars have said that traditional Africans practice "bureaucratic monotheism," or "diffused monotheism," it is clear that they are not monotheists as understood in the scriptures.

8.  We must finally ask, why is there less focus on the Creator God within African traditional understanding? The answer is found in their much stronger focus on humankind. Africa traditional religion is mostly man-centered, or anthropocentric. The central concerns are human health, material and social prosperity, and long life. As Paul says in Romans 1:25, the focus is on the "creature rather than the Creator." There is no concept of a personal relationship with the Creator God, and no teaching about an afterlife of fellowship, joy and peace in heaven. We are left with the conclusion that while Africans have long believed in a single Creator God they still fall very short of Bible truth.

## Questions

1. What does Romans 1:18-32 tell us about what happened to the original revelation of God to our first ancestors, Adam and Eve?

2. Explain what we mean when we say that the Creator God is "hidden" within traditional African religion.

3. Why is idol worship so common within African traditional religion, and what does the Bible say about it?

4. Do you believe traditional African religionists are truly monotheists (believers in one God)? If so, explain. If not, why not?

5. Why is there less focus on God within African traditional religion? Where is the primary focus?

## Things to Think About

❖ *There are few, if any, societies on earth that did not at some point in the past experience a turn from truth to darkness.*

❖ *God has desired to make himself known to people in every age.*

# THE WESTERN PERSPECTIVE

### Ecclesiastes 1:3, 14; Luke 12:19-20

*What profit has a man from all his labor in which he toils under the sun? . . . I have seen all the works that are done under the sun; and indeed, all is vanity and grasping for the wind. . . . I will say to my soul, "Soul, you have many goods laid up for many years; take your ease; eat, drink, and be merry." But God said to him, 'Fool! This night your soul will be required of you; then whose will those things be which you have provided?'*

## Lesson Theme

In this lesson we turn to what can be called both the Western and the secular perspective. We call it Western because it is represented by modern societies living in Europe and the Americas, as well as Australia, New Zealand, India, Israel, Japan and South Korea, etc. The roots of Western society go back for many centuries, but the modern secular perspective of the West was shaped in its present form by the Enlightenment, or 18th-century Rationalism. The result is the ascendancy of human reason and the gradual descendance of belief in the supernatural, including God. Most of the leading voices in Western societies today do not include a strong belief in a supernatural God.

## Introduction

There is no uniform understanding about God within the Western or secular worldview. While Western civilization is heavily based on human reason and scientific thinking and progress, there are many different ways in which God is understood. By its very definition, secularism is the rejection of religion or religious considerations. At its worst it involves outright denial of the existence of God. At its best it demands a complete separation between religion and secular thinking. The result is that some within the Western or secular perspectives accept the reality of a higher being of some kind, yet others do not. In this lesson we will see various ways in which this is played out in our modern world.

## Lesson

1. We use the word "worldview" to refer to how a particular individual or groups of individuals understand the world around them. It is the framework from which they make sense of everything. When we talk about the Western worldview we are referring to a perspective of secularism. As we have already noted, secularism involves the rejection of religion. A secularist excludes the concept of God from his thinking system. He may or may not believe in God,

but in his understanding of the world around him he assumes that God is not involved. He may go to church on Sunday, but on Monday his understanding is that God is not involved in what he is doing or thinking. Instead, human beings now become the measure of all things. This is what we call humanism, which is the valuing of human beings and the accepting of rational thinking rather than religious teaching or belief in the supernatural.

## Western (secular) Worldview

**The Creator God ▶ God**

**( The Spirit World )**

**The Physical World**

animals          man          physical laws

**The Western or secular worldview may or may not leave room for belief in God, but focuses primarily on human beings and the physical world around us.**

1. Within the Western or secular perspective what is believed to be real is only what can be proven with our

five senses (sight, sound, smell, touch and taste) or through our reasoning capacity. Anything beyond that is deemed as either unreal or unprovable, and therefore not to be taken seriously. Within this thinking we say that the universe is a closed system, meaning that everything finds its cause within the existing universe and there are no influences from outside. Thus, even if God might exist somewhere he is withdrawn and is not active in the universe.

2. Another conclusion of secularism is that the spirit world is not to be taken seriously. Secularists do not take seriously the idea of angels and demons, and for the obvious reason that they cannot be proven with our five senses. They cannot be examined in a science laboratory. Even when secularists are presented with evidences of demonic activity the best they can concede is that it is some kind of "parapsychology," or simply unexplained and strange phenomena. Secularists often caricature belief in ghosts, demons, witches, and Satan himself, portraying him as a cartoon figure with horns and wielding a pitchfork.

3. How do secularists view God himself? Here we see more than one answer. Since secularism seeks to exclude religion, the most logical conclusion would be that God does not exist. Indeed, many secularists are atheists. They not only believe that humans are the measure of all things, but they profess to know that God does not exist. The judgment of the Bible on that position, however, is quite clear, as we have already

seen: "The fool has said in his heart, 'There is no God'" (Psalm 14:1; 53:1).

4. Other secularists are not so bold as to make the foolish statement that God does not exist. Instead, they say they are agnostic, meaning that they believe it is impossible to know whether God exists or not. Even if God does exist, they say, no one can say for certain. An honest agnostic certainly deserves more respect than a bold atheist. Yet the agnostic has failed to discover the most important reason for the creation of human beings. God created us for fellowship with himself, meaning that we can both know him and enjoy him, now and throughout all of eternity. The agnostic is still far from God.

5. There are yet other secularists who are theists, and who do believe in the existence of God. But these are people who have chosen to live in a compartmentalized way. They have put their basic understanding of life and how it works in one compartment, and their belief in God in another compartment, and they go back and forth between the two compartments. They are trying to live in two different worlds. They may go to church on Sunday, but when they are back in the science laboratory or the business world or the academic world on Monday they switch from theism to secularism. Much of the Western world operates in this manner. They potentially have a lot to learn from Bible-based Africans.

6. There is something that Western secularism shares with African traditional religious beliefs, and that is that they are human-centered, or anthropocentric. Their primary focus is on the physical world around them, and in particular on the importance of human life and well-being. They are like the rich fool Jesus tells about in Luke 12:16-20. "The ground of a certain rich man yielded plentifully. And he thought within himself, saying, 'What shall I do, since I have no room to store my crops?' So he said, 'I will do this: I will pull down my barns and build greater, and there I will store all my crops and my goods. And I will say to my soul, "Soul, you have many goods laid up for many years; take your ease; eat, drink, *and* be merry."' But God said to him, 'Fool! This night your soul will be required of you; then whose will those things be which you have provided?'

7. What should our response be to this kind of worldly wisdom? Surely it is first to go back to the Bible and find our true foundation there. Second is that we must reaffirm our strong belief in the God of the universe. God is the true measure of all things, and that is what we are going to see clearly in our next lesson.

## Questions

1. When we say the Western perspective is secular what do we mean by "secular"?

2. Within the Western or secular perspective where is the primary focus?

3. What is the difference between an atheist and an agnostic when it comes to belief in God?

4. How would you describe the rich farmer Jesus tells about in Luke 12:16-20?

5. What should our response be to the secularism of the West?

## Things to Think About

❖ *Most of the Western media, as well as Hollywood, is dominated by secular mentality and therefore poisonous to Bible believers.*

❖ *Only a strong belief in the God of the Bible can lead us to ultimate truth that we can depend on.*

# OUR GREAT GOD

# THE BIBLE WORLDVIEW

Psalm 91:1-2; 147:5; Isaiah 40:28

*He who dwells in the secret place of the Most High shall abide under the shadow of the Almighty. I will say of the Lord, "He is my refuge and my fortress; my God, in Him I will trust." . . . Great is our Lord, and mighty in power; His understanding is infinite. . . . Have you not known? Have you not heard? The everlasting God, the Lord, the Creator of the ends of the earth, Neither faints nor is weary. His understanding is unsearchable.*

## Lesson Theme

We have been looking at several perspectives on how people understand God. In this lesson we are coming back to the foundation of our Christian faith, which is the written word of God, the Holy Scriptures. We can debate on and on within ourselves about whether and how God exists, but ultimately, we get our answers from the Bible. We can be sure of what we find within the pages of God Bible. Human reason can fail us. Traditional thinking can leave us deceived and disappointed. But the word of God never fails. Jesus said, "Heaven and earth will pass away, but My word will by no means pass away" (Matthew 24:35). The written word of God is our surest foundation.

## Introduction

When we study the entire Bible, including the thirty-nine books of the Old Testament and the twenty-seven books in the New Testament, we discover the worldview that is behind it. What we discover first and foremost is that the Bible centers around God himself, and then around humankind and their relationship with God. That is why any proper study of the Bible starts with and ends with God. We call it theocentric, or God-centered. That is what we are going to see in this lesson.

## Lesson

1.     As we have said before, the Bible is a theocentric, or God-centered book. It begins with God and it ends with God. The first book of the Bible, Genesis, begins with the words, "In the beginning God . . ." (Gen. 1:1). The last book of the Bible, Revelation, ends with the words, "The grace of our Lord Jesus Christ be with you all. Amen" (Rev. 22:21). Any short summary of the contents of the Bible must include its focus on God and God's search for a relationship with humankind. As we will see, this great God is not only infinite and unfathomable by people, but at the same time he seeks to be near us, to love us, to care for us, and even to listen to us and talk to us. That is the great God of the Bible!

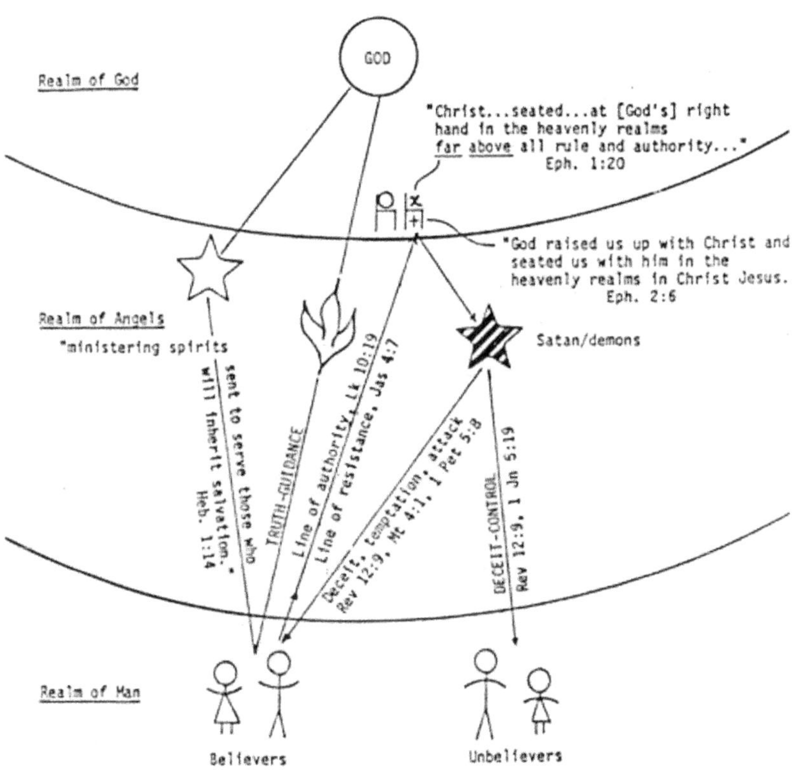


**The Bible worldview has its primary focus on our great God, who is above all, yet with us and constantly seeking to come closer.**

1.  We are beginning to see that the Bible teaches us that God is infinitely greater than we are, and far beyond our feeble understand. Yet it is amazing that at the same time he is on a constant search to come closer to us. We call these two things God's transcendence and his immanence. Transcendence means that he is far above us and beyond our ultimate understanding. In Isaiah

55:8-9 says, "For My thoughts *are* not your thoughts, nor *are* your ways My ways," says the Lord. "For *as* the heavens are higher than the earth, so are My ways higher than your ways, and My thoughts than your thoughts." The immanence of God, however, means that God actually comes down and lives among us and walks with us and talks with us. That was the experience of Adam and Eve, of Abraham, of Enoch, and potentially of all of us today. What a great God we serve!

2. There are many Bible passages that remind us of God's transcendence, in addition to what we have already seen in Isaiah. 1 Timothy 6:15-16 refers to God with these words: *"He who is* the blessed and only Potentate, the King of kings and Lord of lords, who alone has immortality, dwelling in unapproachable light, whom no man has seen or can see, to whom *be* honor and everlasting power." In a similar vein, Romans 11:33-34 says, "Oh, the depth of the riches both of the wisdom and knowledge of God! How unsearchable *are* His judgments and His ways past finding out! "For who has known the mind of the Lord? Or who has become His counselor?"

3. At the same time, however, other Bible passages assure us that God is near to us, and not inaccessible. In his great speech to the Greeks gathered in Athens, Paul declared, "That they should seek God, in the hope that they might feel their way toward him and find him. Yet he is actually not far from each one of us" (Acts 17:27). Psalm 145:18 tells us, "The Lord *is* near to all who call upon Him, to all who call upon Him in truth." Even

more familiar to most of us are the words of Psalm 139:7-10, "Where can I go from Your Spirit? Or where can I flee from Your presence? If I ascend into heaven, You *are* there; if I make my bed in [a]hell, behold, You *are there. If* I take the wings of the morning, a*nd* dwell in the uttermost parts of the sea, even there Your hand shall lead me, and Your right hand shall hold me."

4. What we see again and again throughout the pages of the Bible is that our great God is accessible to humans, and indeed he seeks to be near them. "Enoch walked with God," we are told. Abraham knew him. Moses talked with him. King David sang to him. And so, too, can any of us today. God assured the prophet Jeremiah, "You will seek Me and find *Me,* when you search for Me with all your heart" (Jer. 29:13).

5. When we study the Bible worldview closely we can also see that in addition to a great God who is both transcendent and immanent there is a vast realm of angels that is normally invisible to human eyes. Included in that realm are both the holy angles faithfully serving our great God in worship and communication, and also fallen angels, who have rebelled against Almighty God. Those holy angels wait before God day and night to serve him, and also to act as messengers and guardians over God's faithful followers. We will learn much more about them in a later series of lessons, *The Spirit World.*

6. We have seen that both within the African traditional perspective and in Western secular thinking it is human

beings who are at the center. What we see in the Bible worldview, however, is that the significance or importance of human beings is dependent on their relationship with God. Walking hand-in-hand with God humans can rise to the highest heights imaginable. Paul says that as believers we are seated with Christ in the heavenlies! Without God we are lost. Without God we are nowhere. Even if we gained the whole world we would still lose our soul. The worst possible human fate is to live without God. On the other hand, the greatest possible human achievement is to walk in conscious fellowship with our great God.

7. The most exciting news imaginable is that we have been offered an eternal home in heaven. Heaven is a beautiful place, beyond human imagination, yet the best news is that we have been promised an eternal home in heaven *with God.* In the Qur'an, our Muslim brothers and sisters are told about a wonderful paradise in the afterlife, but without any mention of the presence of God. How sad! By contrast, the Bible says, "Eye has not seen, nor ear heard, nor have entered into the heart of man the things which God has prepared for those who love Him" (1 Cor. 2:9), and Jesus promised his disciples, "I go to prepare a place for you. And if I go and prepare a place for you, I will come again and receive you to Myself; that where I am, *there* you may be also" (John 14:2-3). Thank God for the truth of the Bible about this great God we serve.

## Questions

1. What is the primary focus of the Bible, and what is its secondary focus as well?

2. What do we mean by the transcendence of God and what are some of the scriptures that teach it?

3. What do we mean by the immanence of God and what are some of the scriptures that teach it?

4. Name some examples of God's immanence in the Bible.

5. On what is the significance or importance of human beings dependent?

## Things to Think About

❖ *Without the revelation found in the Bible we might be able to see something of the transcendence of God, but we could have little or no idea of his immanence.*

❖ *If Enoch walked with God so can we.*

# OUR GREAT GOD

# GOD IS A HOLY TRINITY

Matthew 3:16-17; 28:19; Luke 1:35; 2 Corinthians 13:14

*When He had been baptized, Jesus came up immediately from the water; and behold, the heavens were opened to Him, and He saw the Spirit of God descending like a dove and alighting upon Him. And suddenly a voice came from heaven, saying, "This is My beloved Son, in whom I am well pleased." . . . Go therefore and make disciples of all the nations, baptizing them in the name of the Father and of the Son and of the Holy Spirit, . . . And the angel answered and said to her, "The Holy Spirit will come upon you, and the power of the Highest will overshadow you; therefore, also, that Holy One who is to be born will be called the Son of God. . . . The grace of the Lord Jesus Christ, and the love of God, and the [a]communion of the Holy Spirit be with you all. Amen.*

## Lesson Theme

One of the greatest revelations in the Bible about our great God is that God is a Trinity. Though the word "trinity" is not found in the Bible it nevertheless clearly describes a

God who is both three and one. He is the Great Three-in-One. Even in eternity we will never fully understand what it means for God to be three in one, but within the scriptures we can get enough understanding to know that Trinity is a proper description of God. In this lesson we are going to see more about what that means.

## Introduction

The doctrine of the Trinity is found both in the Old Testament and in the New Testament. Right from the first chapter of Genesis we get hints that the Godhead (which is another way of referring to the Trinity) includes the Spirit of God, moving over the waters that God had created (v. 2). Then in verse 26 it says, "Then God said, 'Let *Us* make man in *Our* image, according to *Our* likeness.'" While this is not a clear revelation of Trinity at this point it certainly foreshadows later revelation about it. The action of God the Father is in evidence in the Old Testament. So likewise is that of the Holy Spirit. And we know from the fulfillment of prophecies that the later full revelation of Jesus Christ as the Son of God was revealed through Old Testament prophets such as Isaiah, Micah and Zechariah, among others. It is then when we get to the New Testament that the truth of the Trinity comes through loudly and clearly. Let us study the scriptures and see how all of this unfolds.

## Lesson

1.  The truth that God is both one and three in nature is revealed in the scriptures and was also affirmed in the

early creeds of the Christian Church, such as the Nicene Creed (325 AD). The doctrine of the Trinity is that God is one while at the same time he exists in three eternal Persons: God the Father, God the Son and God the Holy Spirit. The objection that Christians believe in three gods (called tritheism) is often heard from Muslims and others. However, the Bible firmly teaches that there is only one God (Is. 43:10). But the Bible also teaches that the Father is God (John 6:27; 1 Pet. 1:2), the Son is God (John 1:1-3; Tit. 2:13), and the Holy Spirit is God (Acts 5:3-4; 1 Cor. 3:16). Yet these three Persons are distinct from each other, as we see in Matthew 28:19 and Romans 15:20. Much of our problem here is with the use of the word "person," which we normally take to mean distinct and separate existences. However, when used of God we mean that within the one eternal God there are three centers of self-consciousness, but not three separate existences. Each of the three Persons in the Trinity has full possession of the divine nature. It is easy to see how all of this quickly can surpass our human capacity to fully understand. However, for easier understanding we will look at six basic facts about the Trinity as revealed in the Bible.

**The trinity is clearly revealed in the Bible, yet it will always remain beyond full human understanding.**

2. First, as we have noted, the Bible teaches that there is one God, and not two or three or more. The great "shema" of the Old Testament, as frequently repeated by the Jewish people, was, "Hear, O Israel: The Lord our God, the Lord *is* one!" (Deut. 6:4). That there is one God is also clearly taught in the New Testament, such as 1 Timothy 2:5, "For *there is* one God and one Mediator between God and men, *the* Man Christ Jesus."

3. Second, the Bible teaches that God is a Trinity of three Persons. The very first word in the Bible is not "El" (the singular word for "God"), but "Elohim," in the plural (Genesis 1:1). This is not a direct statement of Trinity, but the use of the plural form (as we have already noted in Gen. 1:26) certainly allows for the Trinity. Further, In Isaiah 48:16 and 61:1, God the Son is speaking and

referring to the Father and the Holy Spirit. "The Spirit [Holy Spirit] of the Lord God [the Father] *is* upon Me [Jesus the Son], because the Lord has anointed Me to preach good tidings to the poor." We can recall that these words were quoted by Jesus, as recorded in Luke 4:18, speaking in the synagogue in his boyhood home of Nazareth.

4. Third, we can see by examining various passages of the Bible that each of the Persons of the Trinity operate distinctly, even though God is essentially one. In Psalm 51:10-12 we can see that God the Father is distinct from God the Holy Spirit, as David prays, "Create in me a clean heart, O God, and renew a steadfast spirit within me. Do not cast me away from Your presence, and do not take Your Holy Spirit from me." God speaks in Hebrews 1:8, and says, "But to the Son *He says:* 'Your throne, O God, *is* forever and ever.'" In John 14:16-17 Jesus tells his disciples that he will speak to his Father about the need to send the Holy Spirit: "I will pray the Father, and He will give you another Helper, that He may abide with you forever — the Spirit of truth." In fact, throughout the gospels we hear Jesus repeatedly speaking about and praying to the Father, showing that he and the Father were distinct Persons within the Trinity.

5. Fourth, it is clear from the Bible that each member of the Trinity is fully God. The Father is God ("Grace to you and peace from God our Father" [Rom. 1:7]). The Son is God ("We know that the Son of God . . . is the true God and eternal life" [1 John 5:20]). The Holy

Spirit is God ("Why has Satan filled your heart to lie to the Holy Spirit ?...You have not lied to men but to God" [Acts 5:3-4]).

6. Fifth, we can see that there is some kind of subordination within the Trinity. What we discover by careful reading of the Bible is that the Holy Spirit is subordinate to the Father and the Son (John 14:16; 16:13-14), and that the Son is subordinate to the Father (Luke 22:42; John 5:36). We are not thereby denying the full deity of each Person nor are we denying the oneness of the Godhead. We can only bow our heads in humility and in worship and admit that we cannot fully understand this wonderful Three-in-One Trinity.

7. We can also see, finally, that each Person within the Trinity has peculiar work. God the Father is seen as the ultimate source of creation, though the other two Persons are not absent in that work. The Father is the giver of revelation, the ultimate author of salvation, and the initiator of the incarnation. "For God so loved the world that He gave His only begotten Son, that whoever believes in Him should not perish but have everlasting life. For God did not send His Son into the world to condemn the world, but that the world through Him might be saved" (John 3:16-17). God the Son is the agent through whom the Father creates the word and provides salvation for all humankind. "God was in Christ reconciling the world to Himself" (2 Cor. 5:19). God the Holy Spirit is also the means by which the Father creates, reveals, and applies the redemptive work of the Father and the Son. "According to His

mercy He saved us, through the washing of regeneration and renewing of the Holy Spirit" (Titus 3:5).

8. There are no illustrations that have ever adequately explained the Trinity. Some have suggested the illustration of a chicken egg, consisting of a shell, a yolk and an egg white, yet a single egg. Without any of the parts it is not a real egg. Yet God cannot be divided into separate parts like an egg. Others have suggested the illustration of water, which can be a solid (ice), a liquid, and a gas (vapor). No matter what state it is in it is water. The problem, though, is that water can switch back and forth from solid to liquid to gas, but God does not switch back and forth between Father, Son and Holy Spirit. In the end, we have to admit there are no adequate illustrations. This simple diagram, however, has been used to show the unity and yet the interrelationships between the Father, the Son and the Holy Spirit.

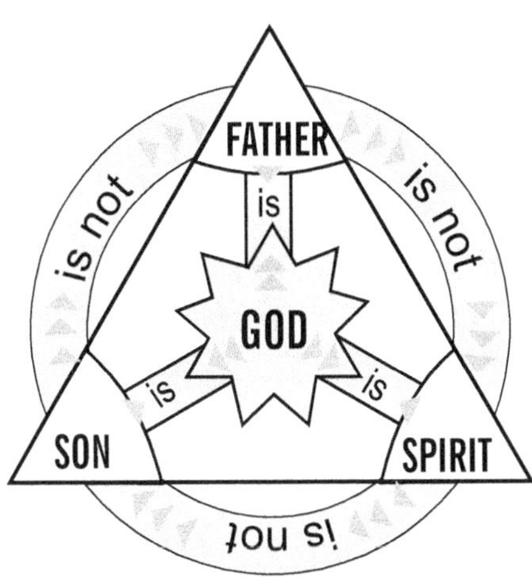

9. Our ultimate privilege as part of the redeemed multitudes of all ages is to simply bow in worship to a great God who is a Holy Trinity. He is God the Father, God the Son, and God the Holy Spirit. We will worship this great God forever in an eternity filled with growing wonder and amazement.

## Questions

1. What hints do we see about the Trinity in the very first chapter in the Bible?

2. Give a definition of "Trinity."

3. What are some of the evidences of the Trinity in the Old Testament?

4. Explain what we mean by subordination within the Trinity.

5. Why is there no illustration that can explain what the Trinity is all about?

## Things to Think About

❖ *"A God comprehended is no God at all."*

❖ *The grace of the Lord Jesus Christ, and the love of God, and the communion of the Holy Spirit be with you all. Amen.* (2 Cor. 13:14)

# MISUNDERSTANDINGS ABOUT THE TRINITY

### 1 John 2:22-23; 4:2-3

*Who is the liar? It is whoever denies that Jesus is the Christ. Such a person is the antichrist — denying the Father and the Son. No one who denies the Son has the Father; whoever acknowledges the Son has the Father also. . . . By this you know the Spirit of God: Every spirit that confesses that Jesus Christ has come in the flesh is of God, and every spirit that does not confess that Jesus Christ has come in the flesh is not of God. And this is the spirit of the Antichrist, which you have heard was coming, and is now already in the world.*

## Lesson Theme

We have seen clearly that the doctrine of the Trinity is well-established within the Bible. At the same time, we have acknowledged that a full understanding of God is never possible by finite human beings. Therefore, it should not surprise us to see that a lot of misunderstandings regarding the Trinity have arisen up over the centuries. It is important for us to understand what some of those misunderstandings are, because most of them are repeated over and over in every generation. Let us be sound in our thinking and in our interpretation of scripture!

## Introduction

The doctrine of the Trinity is at the core of Christian teaching. The Bible is theocentric, and God is a Trinity. In our last lesson we outlined the basic understanding of the Trinity. God is one, but God exists in three Persons. Therefore, God is triune, or three-in-one. However, it should not surprise us that there have been misunderstandings of the Trinity that have persisted down through the ages. Historically the most well-known trinitarian errors historically have been Modalism, Arianism and Tritheism. As we will see in this lesson, Modalists teach that God is not simultaneously Father, Son and Holy Spirit, but only in successive appearances. Arianism teaches that Jesus was not truly God but rather the highest created being of God. Tritheism teaches that there are three separate gods in the Trinity. We shall see that all of these misunderstandings differ from the plain teaching of the Bible.

## Lesson

1. In this lesson we will look first at the three historic trinitarian errors we have mentioned: Modalism, Arianism and Tritheism. All three of them have a long history behind them and all three are still alive today in modern forms of continuing misunderstanding and false teaching. The first is Modalism, which teaches that God is successively Father, Son and Holy Spirit and

never simultaneously Father, Son and Holy Spirit. This is a denial of historic trinitarian doctrine and is embraced in modern times by groups such as Oneness Pentecostals. Oneness Pentecostalism arose in the 1920s and is still alive today and has also been known as the "Jesus Only" movement. The Father, Son and Holy Spirit are not seen as three distinct Persons but as modes or manifestations of one God. Therefore, they teach that God revealed himself in history at times as Father (e.g., in creation), at times as Son (e.g., in redemption), and at other times as Spirit (e.g., in applying the benefits of salvation to believers). For them, Jesus as the Son of God was the manifestation of the Father in a human body. This is false doctrine, It is not consistent with the scriptures or with the historic teachings of the Christian Church.

**Because the trinity is beyond full human understanding we should not be surprised that there have been many false teachings about it.**

2. Arianism is one of the oldest Christian heresies and is still represented today by the teachings of the Jehovah's Witnesses. Original Arianism was founded on the teachings of Arius, who maintained that because God is one Jesus could not have been God. Arius and his followers therefore maintained that Jesus was the highest created being, and that while he was fully human he was not fully God. That teaching was soundly condemned at the Council of Nicaea in 325AD. Yet today Jehovah's Witnesses still teach that Jesus Christ is not God but was rather God's first created being. They identify Jesus with the archangel Michael in the Old Testament. Arianism was wrong 1,700 years ago, and it is still wrong today!

3. Tritheism is the age-old belief that the Trinity is made up of three equal and autonomous beings, each of which is divine. In other words, there are three gods. This is the teaching of modern-day Mormonism. They believe the Trinity involves three separate gods. According to them, the Father is an exalted man who became a god, Jesus is the first spirit-child between God the Father and his wife, and the Holy Spirit is another spirit-child of the Father and his wife. None of these three persons is eternal or almighty God. Moreover, they teach that Jesus and Satan are brothers! We can see that throughout history serious errors have persisted regarding the truth of the Bible about the Trinity.

4. Aside from these historic misunderstandings of the Trinity there are several other common misperceptions. We can only mention a few. One

common idea is that the Trinity does not exist in the Old Testament, and only comes about in the New Testament. However, the truth is that God has always existed as a Trinity, even before the creation of the world. The teaching about the Trinity is a description of the eternal nature of God. God always was and always will be a Trinity.

5. It is not uncommon for people to believe that the Persons within the Trinity are simply forms which God assumes from time to time, and that they are simply different manifestations of one God. As we have noted, this was the error behind Modalism, but it is a popular form of misunderstanding even today among many believers. This kind of misunderstanding is what can happen when people take too literally the illustrations of water or of a chicken egg to which we have referred. Water can exist as vapor, liquid or ice, but it is all water. However, the difficulty with such an explanation is that God exists always and at all times as three Persons: Father, Son and Holy Spirit.

6. Another common misunderstanding of the Trinity is that the Persons within the Trinity operate independently from one another. It is not unusual for us to say that the Father is the creator, Jesus the Son is the Savior, and the Holy Spirit is the sanctifier. These statements are not wrong by themselves, yet in reality we must remember that all of the Persons within the Trinity are One, and therefore they always act in unity. For example, the Father is the Creator, but so also is the

Son (John 1:3; Col. 1:16) and the Holy Spirit (Gen. 1:2; Ps. 104:30).

7. There are some who believe that since the word "trinity" is not in the Bible the teaching of Trinity is not from the Bible but from later teaching, of the Roman Catholic Church. However, from the very first days of the Christian Church believers affirmed the mystery of the Trinity, even without using the word. The Church as a whole has never doubted that God is of one essence and that there are three Persons within the Godhead. The Church has debated how to best express it, but the concept of Trinity is as old as the Bible.

8. Finally, let us note that theology is the human attempt to understand what the Bible teaches us about God and the things of God. Because it is a finite human attempt it will always be flawed to one degree or the other. However, over the centuries the Church has come to articulate what the Bible teaches about God, and the steadfast conclusion is that God has revealed himself and continues to work today as an eternal Trinity. He is indeed our great God!

## Questions

1. Name and define the three most well-known historic misunderstandings of the Trinity.

2. What is the trinitarian error of Oneness Pentecostals who teach a "Jesus Only" theology?

3. What do the Jehovah's Witnesses teach about the Trinity and which ancient heresy are they following?

4. What do the Mormons teach about the Trinity and which ancient heresy are they following?

5. Since the word "trinity" is not in the Bible how can we be sure that the doctrine of the Trinity is scripturally sound?

## Things to Think About

❖ *Most of those who follow modern heretical groups such as the Jehovah's Witnesses and the Mormons are unaware that the Christian Church long ago rejected their basic teachings as false and anti-Bible.*

❖ *The best way to detect false doctrines is to become a more faithful student of the Bible.*

# OUR GREAT GOD

52

# GOD IS INFINITE

Job 36:22-23; Isaiah 55:9; Ephesians 1:18-19

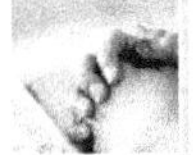

*"Behold, God is exalted by His power; who teaches like Him? Who has assigned Him His way, or who has said, 'You have done wrong'? ... "For as the heavens are higher than the earth, so are My ways higher than your ways, and My thoughts than your thoughts....the eyes of your understanding being enlightened; that you may know what is the hope of His calling, what are the riches of the glory of His inheritance in the saints, and what is the exceeding greatness of His power toward us who believe, according to the working of His mighty power.*

## Lesson Theme

We have continually reminded ourselves in these lessons that our great God is beyond fully accurate human description and full human understanding. However, this same God invites us to come near and to know him as much as possible, and especially through Jesus Christ, our Lord and Savior. Paul said to the Philippians, "I also count all things loss for the excellence of *the knowledge of Christ*

*Jesus my Lord, . . . that I may know Him* and the power of His resurrection, and the fellowship of His sufferings" (Phil. 3:8, 10). We have said, however, that the major barrier that prevents our full understanding of our great God is that we are finite creatures and our God is truly infinite. In this lesson we will attempt to understand exactly what we mean when we say that God is infinite.

## Introduction

There are a number of words we use to describe the infinite nature of God. We say, for example, that he is omnipresent, by which we mean that he is present everywhere. There is no place where God does not exist. We say that he omniscient, by which we mean that he knows everything. Nothing is hidden from God's knowledge or secret to his understanding. We also say that he is omnipotent, meaning that he is all-powerful. There is no power in the universe that is not derived from God and that does not operate within boundaries set by God. Closely related to God's omnipotence is his omnificence, which refers to God's unlimited ability for creation. We also sometimes say that God is omnibenevolent. By that we are asserting that God is always good. There is nothing about him that is not pure, righteous and good. In this lesson we will look at each of these descriptions of God's infinite nature. When we take into our minds this entire picture we surely can and most bow our heads in deep reverence and way that we serve a great God.

## Lesson

1. When we talk about an infinite God we refer to the fact that he has no limits. However, we also steer away from the error of pantheism, which denies the personality or distinct existence of God and instead assumes that God is the sum total of the universe. For pantheists everything is God, and God is everything. That was true before God created anything, but creation is a reality and God is separate from his creation, though he is the ultimate source of everything beyond himself. God exists apart from his creation, yet he is unlimited and unmeasurable. He is the source of everything else. The best way the Bible describes him is by calling him the great "I AM" (Ex. 3:14). We also note that God is a being, as we see in Genesis 1:26-27. He is personal, and that is why he can reveal himself to us within the limits of our capacity to receive it. It is why God not only wants to know us, but longs to have a relationship with us.

**Our great God is mightier and greater than the universe. He created everything that exists, and he surpasses it all!**

2. When we think of the infinity of God often the first thing that comes to our minds is his omnipresence: God is present everywhere. We are familiar with the question of the psalmist, "Where can I go from Your Spirit? Or where can I flee from Your presence?" (Ps. 139:7). God's presence can sometimes be in a manifest manner that we are quite aware of. Psalm 46:1 says, "God is our refuse and strength, a very present help in trouble." But whether or not we are aware, God is present in every situation, at every time and throughout all of creation. "The Lord looks from heaven; He sees all the sons of men" (Ps. 33:13). It is true that our sins can separate us from God (Is. 52:9). There is also a sense in which he is far from the wicked (Prov. 15:29). Yet that separation does not mean God is not there at all, but that we have created a barrier making it impossible to know or enjoy or respond to his presence.

3. There are two special theological words related to this question about God's omnipresence: transcendence and immanence. These are important words because they help us understand our great God better. The word "transcendent" means above, beyond, or surpassing. God is greater than all things. He is beyond them and above them, yet he also sustains them by his own power (Heb. 1:3). Paul says of God, "How unsearchable *are* His judgments and His ways past finding out!" (Rom. 11:33). Yet God also seeks to be known. He seeks to reveal himself to us. He wants us to seek him. "Seek the Lord while He may be found, call upon Him while He is near" (Is. 55:6). It is a paradox:

The God who can never be fully known wants us to know him as much as possible. That is why he walked with Adam and Eve in the Garden of Eden, why he walked with Enoch, why he walked with Abraham and with Moses, why Jesus walked with his disciples, and why all of us today can walk with God in our own lives. He is transcendent, but he is also immanent, or near at hand.

4. Another aspect of God's infinity is his eternity. By that we mean that he has no beginning and no end. As human beings we will live for all of eternity, yet we all had a beginning and there was a time when we were not. God, however, is the only being who exists from all eternity past to all eternity future. "Before the mountains were brought forth, or ever You had formed the earth and the world, even from everlasting to everlasting, You *are* God" (Ps. 90:2). Jewish leaders were prepared to stone Jesus for blasphemy when he said, "Before Abraham was, I AM" (John 8:58). He was pointing to the fact that as God he had always existed.

5. Because God is omnipresent (present everywhere) he is also *omniscient*, meaning he know everything. He has all knowledge. "God is greater than our heart, and *knows all things*" (1 John 3:20). Jesus reminded us that God knows even when a single hair falls out of our heads (Matt. 10:29-30). He knows the past, the present and the future, including everything that will happen at the end of history here on earth (Is. 46:9-10). God knows the innermost secrets of our hearts (Acts 1:24). Even during Jesus' ministry, in which he had voluntarily

taken on some limitations in order to experience human nature in its fullness, Jesus knew all about the former life of the woman at the well (John 4), about the fish with the coin in its mouth (Matt. 17:27), etc. God is truly all-knowing.

6. Our great God is also omnipotent. He is all-powerful. God has power over all things. Job said, "I know that You can do everything, and that no purpose *of Yours* can be withheld from You" (Job 42:2). Genesis 1 shows the awesome display of God's power in bringing the universe into existence merely by speaking a word. "By the word of the Lord were the heavens made" (Ps. 33:6). It is through the power of God that the universe continues its God-appointed course, and in such a way that human life is wonderfully sustained. God even displays his power over human governments (Dan. 2:21), and he puts limits on what men, angels and demons can do. He has purposefully allowed free will to people, which means he has allowed evil to exist at least for a season. Jesus noted that even if his body were destroyed, he would raise it again in three days (John 2:19). God is truly all-powerful, and he invites us as believers to share in that power. This is why Paul reminds us that God is "able to do exceedingly abundantly above all that we ask or think, according to the power that works in us" (Eph. 3:20).

7. Our great God is also omnificent and omnibenevolent. Those are two words with which we may be less familiar. "Omnificent" means that God has the ability to create anything he wants. The Bible begins with the

words, "In the beginning God created" (Gen. 1:1). "In him all things were created" (Col 1:15-17). And God is also omnibenevolent, meaning that he is eternally and infinitely good. There is no action or attitude or thought of God that is not pure and righteous and good. The presence of evil in the world has sometimes caused people to doubt the ultimate goodness of God. We may not be able to fully understand the problem of evil in the world, but we can rest assured that even to sinners God's word is "good news" (Luke 2:10). It is the goodness of God that leads us to repentance (Rom. 2:4). The psalmist says, "Praise the Lord! Oh, give thanks to the Lord, for *He is* good! For His mercy *endures* forever" (Ps. 106:1).

8. We worship a great God who is truly infinite. He has no limits. Our tiny minds will never grasp all that it means, yet we know we are safe in the hands of an all-powerful, ever-present, all-knowing and all-good God. He is truly and forever our great God!

## Questions

1. What is the difference between the teaching of pantheism and the Bible teaching of the infinity of God?

2. What do we mean by the transcendence and the immanence of God?

3. What is the difference between the eternal life of believers and the eternity of God himself?

4. Explain the omniscience of God and give some examples of it.

5. The Bible says that God cannot lie (Num. 23:19; Heb. 6:18). Does that mean that he is not omnipotent?

## Things to Think About

❖ *We can all enjoy the gift of eternal life and the awareness that we will live forever with God, but we will never share his quality of eternity.*

❖ *Surrendering our lives to the infinite God is the smartest thing humans can ever do.*

# PART TWO

# GOD THE FATHER

We have looked at some of the important general descriptions of God, including a look at the reality of the Trinity. God is three-in-one, or triune. He exists as one God, complete and consistent in his unity. Yet he also exists in three Persons: God the Father, God the Son and God the Holy Spirit. In this second part of our studies we will look at what the Bible teaches us about God the Father.

The fatherhood of God is taught on both the Old Testament and in the New Testament. Following the guidance of Jesus, most Christians refer to God as their heavenly Father when they pray. Yet even in the Old Testament the nation of Israel understood that Yahweh was their Father.

In this second part of our study of God we will see that the most common perception of God, both in the Bible and among most believers today, is that he is our Heavenly Father. We know that God is a trinity, yet our most common perception is that he is watching over us and caring for us as a father.

# OUR GREAT GOD

# GOD AS CREATOR

Genesis 1:1; Isaiah 40:28; Colossians 1:15-17

*In the beginning God created the heavens and the earth. . . . Have you not known? Have you not heard? The everlasting God, the Lord, the Creator of the ends of the earth, neither faints nor is weary. His understanding is unsearchable. . . . He is the image of the invisible God, the firstborn over all creation. For by Him all things were created that are in heaven and that are on earth, visible and invisible, whether thrones or dominions or principalities or powers. All things were created through Him and for Him. And He is before all things, and in Him all things consist.*

## Lesson Theme

One of the most universal beliefs held throughout the African continent is that God is the creator of everything that exists, including human beings. Our scripture lesson from Isaiah 40:28 says it boldly, "Have you not known? Have you not heard? The everlasting God, the Lord, the Creator of the ends of the earth, neither faints nor is weary." It is no mistake that the Bible starts with the existence of the eternal God ("In the beginning God") and then immediately moves to the foundational truth that he created the entire universe ("created the heavens and the earth"). Then as we dig deeper into the scriptures we eventually discover that the creation of the universe involved all three Persons of the Trinity. God the Father is clearly there, but we see the Holy Spirit as well in Genesis 1:2 ("The Spirit of God was hovering over the face of the waters"). Hebrews 1:1-2 expressed the involvement of God the Son: "God . . . has in these last days spoken to us by *His* Son, whom He has appointed heir of all things, through whom also He made the worlds." In this lesson we will see why the engagement of God in creation is so important for our faith.

## Introduction

Secular scientists have struggled for many years to try to explain the existence of the universe. Though they are reluctant to concede the existence of an eternal God, they have repeatedly come up against the impossibility of a physical universe without an ultimate creator. Many years ago, when astronomers discovered that the universe is expanding, they promoted the theory that it all started with a Big Bang at a singular point, in the very distant past. The problem, however, is that they were reluctant to speculate about Who "banged" the Big Bang. It was evident that there had to be a First Cause, as philosophers would say. What the secular scientists did not realize was that they could have saved a lot of time, energy and laboratory expense by simply opening their Bibles to Genesis 1:1, which has the most imaginably simple statement ever made about creation: "In the beginning God created the heavens and the earth." That is the truth that we must pursue in this lesson. It is all the doing of our great God!

## Lesson

1.  When we talk about creation it is important to note the difference between God's acts of creation and those of human beings. To create something means to make something new that did not exist previously. Human beings create music, or other works of art, beautiful buildings, roads, delicious food, or gardens. But this is not the same as when God creates. Humans create by bringing together materials which are already there. But when God created the heavens and the earth there were no previous materials with which to work. When God creates he is in a category totally his own, because God starts with nothing. Colossians 1:16 says, "For by Him all things were created that are in heaven and that are on earth, visible and invisible, whether thrones or dominions or principalities or powers. All things were created through Him and for Him." Before his creation there was no previously-existing matter. That is true divine creation.

**How an infinite God can create the vast universe is more than we can understand. He is surely a great God!**

2. Those who accept modern theories of atheistic naturalism believe that everything in the universe arose by natural causes, without the engagement of any divine powers. They say that time and chance not only brought the universe into existence but that it resulted in the gradual evolution of the world right down to our own day. Such thinking is obviously foolish. We have repeated the psalmist's cry already, but we must repeat it again: "The fool has said in his heart: 'There is no God'" (Ps. 14;1; 53:1). The Bible is clear that God is the creator, and that right from the beginning he established the earth, the sky, the planets, stars and galaxies, and that he created man, animals and plants each according to their own species. We serve an incredible creator God!

3. There are still many unanswered questions we may have regarding the first eleven chapters of Genesis. What we know is that with Genesis 12 we start the story

of the national of Israel, beginning with their first ancestor, Abraham. Abraham lived 2,000 years before Christ. Yet prior to Abraham, in chapters 1 11, we have the long, long stretch of time from the creation of the world to Abraham. It was at least 2,000 years and possibly much more. We see the creation of Adam and Eve, and then eventually the emergence of entire nations. We see the great flood and the heroic actions of Noah. Through all of it God, the great creator, was moving to call out and form his own people and prepare the pathway for the coming of the Messiah.

4. Going back to Genesis 1, we see that God demonstrated his unique powers by creating something out of nothing. Theologians call is *creatio ex nihilo* ("creation out of nothing"). In ancient Greek mythologies creation was always depicted as bringing order out of chaos, and never as creating the world from nothing. But this is exactly what is stated in Genesis 1:1. Before then there was no earth and there were no heavens. There was nothing but God himself. Hebrews 11:3 further notes, "By faith we understand that the worlds were framed by the word of God, so that the things which are seen were not made of things which are visible." Further, John describes the twenty-four elders in Revelation 4:11 who echo praise to God as a Creator ex nihilo - "You are worthy, O Lord, to receive glory and honor and power; for You created all things, and by Your will they exist and were created."

5. But how did God actually go about creation? We have seen in Hebrews 11:3 that "the worlds were framed *by*

*the word of God.*" In Genesis 1:3, 6, 9 we see that God spoke the world into existence ("Then God said . . ."). Theologians say, therefore, that God created by divine *fiat*, i.e., by merely speaking the word. "Let all the earth fear the Lord; let all the inhabitants of the world stand in awe of Him. For He spoke, and it was *done;* He commanded, and it stood fast" (Ps. 33:8-9).

6. However, when we talk about the creation of human beings by the great Creator God we see some remarkable differences. In the creation of Adam God took some of the clay he had already created and formed it into a man. He then "breathed into his nostrils the breath of life; and man became a living being" (Gen. 2:7). Likewise, when he created the first woman he took something he had already made. "He took one of [Adam's] ribs, and . . . the rib which the Lord God had taken from man He made into a woman" (2:21-22). All this tells us that human beings are well above the rest of creation. They were made in the image of God (Gen. 1:26-27) and it was symbolized by the breath of God breathed into them. Human beings have an eternal spirit, and will live forever, just as God will. We can make free choices, for good or for evil, and we can love God. God created us for fellowship with himself. He does not fellowship with elephants and dogs or with the trees of the forest. They do not have the life of God within them.

7. We must note also that because God is the creator of the heavens and the earth and of everything in them,

including human beings, he is therefore the rightful owner of it all. The psalmist rightly sings, "The earth *is* the Lord's, and all its fullness, the world and those who dwell therein" (Ps. 24:1-2). "For every beast of the forest *is* Mine, a*nd* the cattle on a thousand hills. . . . For the world *is* Mine, and all its fullness" (Ps. 50:10, 12). If a master artist creates a great painting the product is his own property unless and until he sells or assigns it to someone else. And since God created the heavens and the earth, and you and me, he is the rightful owner of it all. He is truly a great God.

8.   Finally, we must note that God has not concluded his work of creation. He is still creating today. Jesus told his disciples that he was going away to continue his work of creation. "In My Father's house are many mansions; if *it were* not *so,* I would have told you. I go to prepare a place for you" (John 14:2). In confirmation of this promise, John tells us in Revelation 21:4-5, "And God will wipe away every tear from their eyes; there shall be no more death, nor sorrow, nor crying. There shall be no more pain, for the former things have passed away." Then He who sat on the throne said, '*Behold, I make all things new*'" (Rev. 21:4-5). It is by remaining true to our great God and Creator that we, too, can experience one day his new creation.

## Questions

1. What evidence do we have that all three Persons of the Trinity were involved in creation?

2. How can we describe the difference between creation of men and the creation of the world by God?

3. What do we mean by *creatio ex nihilo*? Explain how that is described in the Bible.

4. What are the differences between how God created the plants and animals and how he created human beings?

5. How has God gained the right of ownership over the entire universe, and what are the implications for we human beings?

**Things to Think About**

❖ *For many atheists the problem is not so much that they do not believe in the existence of God but that they do not like the God they believe may actually be there.*

❖ *We can learn much about the greatness of God merely by peering into our telescopes and into our powerful microscopes to get a better picture of his incredible universe.*

# GOD AS REVEALED IN THE OLD TESTAMENT

### Psalm 19:1; 1 Timothy 6:15-16; Hebrews 11:1-2

*And they heard the sound of the Lord God walking in the garden in the cool of the day, and Adam and his wife hid themselves from the presence of the Lord God among the trees of the garden. Then the Lord God called to Adam and said to him, "Where are you?" So he said, "I heard Your voice in the garden, and I was afraid because I was naked; and I hid myself." . . . And I will establish My covenant between Me and you and your descendants after you in their generations, for an everlasting covenant, to be God to you and your descendants after you. . . . For I know the thoughts that I think toward you, says the Lord, thoughts of peace and not of evil, to give you a future and a hope.*

## Lesson Theme

We said at the beginning of Part One that the Bible is a theocentric, or a God-centered book. It begins with God and ends with God. Right from the beginning of Genesis we start to discover many things about this great God. There are some people who like to distribute New

Testaments, without the Old Testament as well. Yet it is a mistake to believe that we can grasp all that God wants us to know about himself, about his creation, about the origins of human life and their subsequent fall into sin and God's covenants with them, without holding the Old Testament with the same care and love with which we regard the New Testament. That is why in this lesson we are going to ask the question about what we learn about God through the pages of the Old Testament.

## Introduction

The mystery of who God is and how we as finite humans can understand an infinite God is seen throughout the pages of the Old Testament. Even when we see God in action we often still have unanswered questions: What does it really mean to hear God speak? How does such communication relate to my own experiences of God? Were some of the men and women of the Old Testament closer to God than is possible for people who are living in our own day? What does it mean in Exodus 33 where we read about Moses seeing God's back? There are many such questions we can raise, and the truth is that we cannot always find answers that are completely satisfying to us. Yet it is also true that we can learn much about God through the revelation of the Old Testament, and that is what we are examining in this lesson. We will see that God has not left us without a great witness to who he is and what his intentions are for us as well.

## Lesson

1. We have already seen that one of the greatest revelations about God in the Old Testament is that he is the Creator God. He not only created the heavens and the earth (Gen. 1:1), but he also created human beings, in his own image (Gen. 1:26-27). In order for God to be the creator of the heavens and the earth we also therefore know that he is an infinite, eternal and all-powerful God. As Creator God he knows everything, and he is present in all of his creation. Nothing speaks louder about the greatness of our God than the fact that he is the source of everything else that exists.

**God revealed himself to Moses more than to any other person in the Old Testament, starting with his encounter with a burning bush, in Exodus 3.**

2. The second thing we discover in the Old Testament is that God is a personal God who continually seeks for

relationship with human beings. This is the secret behind the fact that God created human beings in his own image. We are image-bearers. As theologians say it, we were created in the *imago dei*, the image of God. What that means first and foremost is that we, of all God's creation, are the ones who can have a free relationship with himself in which we enjoy real two-way communication.

3. Adam and Eve, our first parents, enjoyed a wonderful relationship with the Creator God which we can only imagine. The Bible says they walked with God "in the cool of the day" (Gen. 3:8). Yet we also discover that before long sin entered into the world and became a huge barrier to the relationship for which God has created us. However, God did not relent in his original purpose. The rest of the Bible shows us that God seeks to bring sinful and fallen human beings into relationship with himself through grace. He wants to restore the lost fellowship for which we were created, and he can achieve that only by dealing with the curse of sin. Light cannot fellowship with darkness. Evil cannot fellowship with righteousness. God therefore calls out, "Be holy, because I am holy" (Lev. 19:2; 1 Pet. 1:15-16). In short, we learn through both the Old Testament and the New Testament that God is a God of relationship and he seeks to know us in close harmony and relationship, on the basis of shared character.

4. We discover also that Yahweh (the personal name of God) is a God of covenant. In order to bring about and maintain the restored relationship with human beings

that is so important both for God and them, there must be a covenant. A covenant within the Old Testament is in the form of an agreement between two very unequal partners. God is sovereign and infinite, yet he wants to strike an agreement with finite and faltering people. He therefore repeatedly seeks covenants, with Noah, with Abraham, with Moses, etc. In his covenants God makes firm promises, including protection, life, prosperity, etc. He then bases the fulfillment of the covenants on the response of human beings, including things such as obedience, faith, and righteousness. That an infinite God can make covenant with finite and helpless people is one of the great and exciting mysteries of the Bible.

5. We also learn in the Old Testament that Yahweh is a God of justice. This is why the problem of sin and rebellion is never taken lightly by God. He has established an eternal principle that "The soul who sins shall die" (Ezek. 8:20), as echoed also in Romans 6:23, "The wages of sin is death." Therefore, the justice of God demands that a penalty must be paid for sin. Throughout the Old Testament this is why animal sacrifices were demanded, so that it would be clear to all that God takes sin with utmost seriousness and cannot either excuse it or allow it to go unpunished. It would mean that God had to send his only begotten Son, Jesus Christ, to be the eternal sacrifice for sin and thereby satisfy God's justice.

6. This leads us to understand that Yahweh is revealed in the Old Testament also as a God of mercy. God repeatedly withholds his just condemnation and does

so ultimately through the sending of his one and only Son, Jesus Christ, to stand in our place. We can see clearly that God loves to forgive repentant sinners. God yearns to be reconciled to wayward people. He loves to show mercy, yet he always does so within the context of the covenant he makes with human beings. The examples of God's mercy in the Old Testament are many, including the rescue of Israel from Egyptian bondage, the sending of the Prophet Nathan to sinful King David, etc. The psalmist says over and over, "His mercy endures forever" (Ps. 136:1-26).

7.  God is revealed also as a God of love. There are many places where that love is described in the Old Testament. Nehemiah 9:17b, for example, says, "You *are* God, ready to pardon, gracious and merciful, slow to anger, abundant in kindness." God demonstrated his love to Nineveh in the Book of Jonah, after the people of Nineveh repented of their sins: "God saw their works, that they turned from their evil way; and God relented from the disaster that He had said He would bring upon them, and He did not do it" (Jonah 3:10). Yahweh also assured Isaiah, "'Though the mountains be shaken and the hills be removed, yet my unfailing love for you will not be shaken nor my covenant of peace be removed,' says the Lord, who has compassion on you" (Is. 54:10 NIV).

8.  As we have seen in Lesson Five, God is a Trinity and he is revealed as such even in the Old Testament. Right from the first chapter of Genesis we begin to get hints that the Godhead (which is another way of referring to

the Trinity) includes the Spirit of God, moving over the waters that God had created (v. 2). Verse 26 says, "Then God said, 'Let *Us* make man in *Our* image, according to *Our* likeness.'" While this is not a clear revelation of Trinity at this point it certainly foreshadows later revelation about it. The action of God the Father is in evidence in the Old Testament. So likewise is that of the Holy Spirit. And we know from the fulfillment of prophecies that the later full revelation of Jesus Christ as the Son of God was revealed through Old Testament prophets such as Isaiah, Micah and Zechariah, among others. It is then when we get to the New Testament that the truth of the Trinity comes through more loudly and clearly.

9. Hopefully we can see how important it is for us to cherish the revelation that God has given us both in the Old Testament and in the New Testament. The richness of the descriptions of our great God in the Old Testament should be a cherished part of our theology. He, and he alone, is worthy of our most serious devotion and worship.

## Questions

1. What do we mean when we say that God is a relational being, and what are the implications for human beings?

2. What is the significance of covenants in the Old Testament and why are they important to both God and people?

3. How is the justice of God to be understood in the light of sin?

4. What are some examples of God's mercy in the Old Testament?

5. How is the love of God revealed in the Old Testament?

## Things to Think About

❖ *Without the revelation of the Old Testament our understanding of God would be greatly diminished.*

❖ *The gospel that is revealed in the New Testament can only make sense on the foundation of God's earlier revelation in the Old Testament.*

# THE FATHER AS REVEALED IN THE OLD TESTAMENT

### Exodus 4:22-23; Isaiah 63:16; Hosea 11:1; Malachi 2:10

 *Then you shall say to Pharaoh, 'Thus says the Lord: "Israel is My son, My firstborn. So I say to you, let My son go that he may serve Me. But if you refuse to let him go, indeed I will kill your son, your firstborn."'" . . . Doubtless You are our Father, though Abraham was ignorant of us, and Israel does not acknowledge us. You, O Lord, are our Father; our Redeemer from Everlasting is Your name. . . . "When Israel was a child, I loved him, and out of Egypt I called My son. . . .Have we not all one Father? Has not one God created us?*

## Lesson Theme

There are several ways in which the concept of God as Father is understood within the scriptures. We acknowledge right away that the use of the word "father" is accommodating our human language in our attempt to understand a great and often unfathomable God. It is what we call anthropomorphic language, or describing God in human terms, even though he is not human. We all know what it means to be a father in our human experience. A human father provides, guides, protects, disciplines and is responsible for his children. As the creator of the heavens and the earth and everything that is in them, God is the father over it all. Yet we also discover in the Old Testament that in a more specific sense Yahweh was the Father of the nation of Israel. Israel was his son (Jer. 31:20). When we move to the New Testament we discover that Jesus of Nazareth, the promised Messiah, has a unique relationship with his heavenly Father, and then he invites his disciples to enter into that relationship themselves, by teaching them to pray when addressing God by beginning with the words, "Our Father" (Mat. 6:9). In this lesson we will see how the fatherhood of God is revealed especially in the Old Testament.

## Introduction

We have already seen that the doctrine of the Trinity is clearly supported by the Bible. However, it is seen most clearly in the New Testament and only dimly within the pages of the Old Testament. Because the presence and reality of the incarnate Son of God is not revealed in its full clarity until the birth of Jesus in Bethlehem, it is only after that point that we can see clearly the relationship of Jesus as the Son with God the Father. However, the foundation for the fatherhood of God is clearly laid in the pages of the Old Testament, and that is what we want to see as clearly as possible in this lesson. There is an important sense in which God is the Father of all creation by virtue of his creative actions. As we move forward in the Book of Genesis, with the emergence of Abraham and the other patriarchs, we begin to see that God is also in a much more specific sense the Father of the nation of Israel. That fatherhood is eventually to be shared by all who will eventually participate in the faith of our Father Abraham. We are the children of God, and he is our loving Heavenly Father.

## Lesson

It is clear from the scriptures that God is the creator of all people. In that sense he can rightly be seen as their father. All of humanity can cry out the prayer of Isaiah 64:8, "But now, O Lord, You are our Father; we are the clay, and You our potter; and all we are the work of Your hand." Yet it is also true that in the Old Testament it is Israel that is singled out as the unique "son" of God. Hosea 11:1 says, very simply, "Out of Egypt I called My son," referring to the children of Israel. Exodus 4:22 says similarly, "Israel is My son, My firstborn." Therefore, it is to Israel first and foremost that God is a Father. He is rightfully their Father because it is God who promised, planned and orchestrated the great Exodus from Egyptian slavery through which he then created a great nation that was to change the course of history and that still has impact on world affairs more than 3,000 years later.

**Yahweh is described throughout the Old Testament as the Father of his people Israel. He is the Father of all creation.**

2.  We see the concept of the fatherhood of God also in the fact that God himself numerous times refers to his entire creation as his "children." "Hear, O heavens, and give ear, O earth! For the Lord has spoken: 'I have nourished and brought up children, and they have rebelled against Me,'" (Is. 1:2). In Exodus 4:22,23 Yahweh instructs Moses to go back to Egypt and speak to Pharaoh and tell him, "'Thus says the Lord: "Israel *is* My son, My firstborn. So I say to you, let My son go that he may serve Me.'" God the Father speaks to his human creation also in Psalm 82:6, saying, "All of you *are* children of the Most High."

3.  References to God as Father are particularly clear in the writing of the Old Testament prophets. Isaiah 63:16 says, "Doubtless You *are* our Father, though Abraham was ignorant of us, and Israel does not acknowledge us. You, O Lord, *are* our Father." Jeremiah echoes the same

refrain: "For I am a father to Israel, and Ephraim is my firstborn" (Jer. 31:9), and "You shall call me, My father; and shall not turn away from me" (Jer. 3:19)

4. The last book of the Old Testament, Malachi, has several references to God as Father. "If I then am the Father, where is My honor" (Mal. 1:6). "Have we not all one Father? Has not one God created us?" (Mal. 2:10) The Jewish writings during the intertestamental period between Malachi and Matthew also contain many references to God as "Our Father." The Jewish wise man Ben Sira, writing 200 years before Jesus, prayed "O Lord, Father and Master of my life. . . . O Lord, Father and God of my life" (Ben Sira 23:1, 4).

5. The fatherhood of God is closely related in the Bible to the doctrine of salvation. A father is someone who loves and cares for his children and who gives out his own resources to assist them. Within the Old Testament narrative, the most outstanding event, which is still celebrated today by the Jewish people, is the Passover and the Exodus. It is a paradigm of salvation. The Exodus from Egyptian slavery was the act of the Father God graciously bringing salvation to his people Israel. We have seen it already: "When Israel was a child, I loved him, and out of Egypt I called My son" (Hosea 11:1). In the light of the later revelation of the New Testament we can see the picture of salvation even more clearly: God the Father planned our salvation, God the Son executed it, and God the Holy Spirit applies it to our lives. Yet it all started in the mind of God the Father.

6. When we get to the New Testament we now see the fatherhood of God referenced repeatedly as Jesus refers to God as the Father. He frequently refers to "my Father," and when the disciples implore him to teach them to pray he instructs them to begin their own prayers with the words, "Our Father in heaven" (Matt. 6:9). Jesus is teaching his followers that God is not only the father of Israel, but that he is his own father, and he also the father of all who call on his name.

## Questions

1. What is anthropomorphic language, and how does it apply in this lesson to our understanding of God?

2. Why is it proper for us to refer to God as the Father of all people?

3. What is the primary application of the fatherhood of God within the Old Testament? Of whom is he most frequently referred to as Father?

4. How is the fatherhood of God related to the Bible doctrine of salvation?

5. How is the doctrine of the fatherhood of God applied in a new way in the New Testament?

## Things to Think About

❖ *It is by looking at God and understanding his relationship to humanity that we can understand more deeply what it means to be a human father.*

❖ *God deeply desires that all people everywhere know him intimately as their heavenly Father.*

# GOD IS OUR FATHER

Psalm 25:5; Isaiah 64:8; 1 Peter 1:3-5

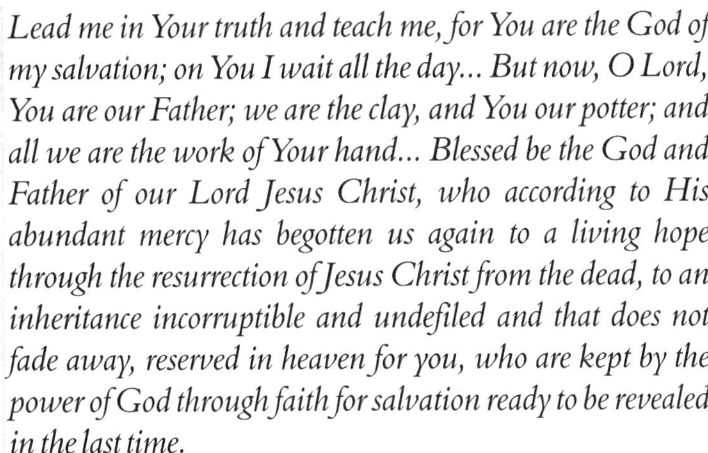

*Lead me in Your truth and teach me, for You are the God of my salvation; on You I wait all the day... But now, O Lord, You are our Father; we are the clay, and You our potter; and all we are the work of Your hand... Blessed be the God and Father of our Lord Jesus Christ, who according to His abundant mercy has begotten us again to a living hope through the resurrection of Jesus Christ from the dead, to an inheritance incorruptible and undefiled and that does not fade away, reserved in heaven for you, who are kept by the power of God through faith for salvation ready to be revealed in the last time.*

## Lesson Theme

We have seen in previous lessons that the Bible clearly portrays God as the Father of all creation, and particularly as the Father of the nation Israel and the Father of our Lord and Savior, Jesus Christ. In this lesson we are focusing on what it means for Christian believers to have a heavenly Father. What are the characteristics of our great God that we can see in his role as our Father? Hopefully when we consider the role of an ideal human father we can then quickly acknowledge that God our heavenly Father surpasses that ideal in every respect.

## Introduction

The most obvious element of truth that is missing within the teachings of African Traditional Religion is the role of God not simply as Creator but as a loving Heavenly Father. Sadly, nothing like that exists within ATR. For traditional Africans, God is almost always understood to be remote and inaccessible. Therefore, direct worship of God is seldom seen within African Traditional Religion. Instead, worship is most often directed to intermediaries, and in the process, there are often elements of uncertainty, fear and foreboding. Not so, however, when we open our Bibles and learn about Yahweh, the Creator of the heavens and the earth. We discover that he is not only mighty and unfathomably superior to us, but that he is also a heavenly Father who yearns to know us in a personal relationship. We cannot ignore the fact that the Bible talks about our need to fear God, but the meaning there is not terror before an unpredictable tyrant, but awe before an infinitely powerful being, who also truly loves us and wills our best. Truly we serve a great God! We will see in this lesson the ways in which God is very much like a father. He is, in fact, our Heavenly Father.

## Lesson

1. The first sense in which we can proclaim God as our father is that he is fully responsible for our very existence. Earthly fathers are responsible for the existence of their children, and to an even greater extent God is responsible for our existence, as our Creator. Isaiah 64:8 tells us, "But now, O Lord, You *are* our Father; we *are* the clay, and You our potter; and all we *are* the work of Your hand." Knowing that without the will and action of God none of us would have ever come into their world, we owe deep gratitude to our Heavenly Father. Psalm 139:13-14 expresses it very clearly: "For You formed my inward parts; You covered me in my mother's womb. I will praise You, for I am fearfully *and* wonderfully made; Marvelous are Your works, and *that* my soul knows very well."

**The fatherhood of God is a familiar metaphor for us because of our own experiences of fatherhood.**

2. A second and profound reason why God is our Father is that he not only created us, but he also provided our salvation after we had fallen away into sin and disobedience. He saved us. The psalmist cried out, "He [God] inclined to me, and heard my cry. He also brought me up out of a horrible pit, out of the miry clay, and set my feet upon a rock, *and* established my steps" (Psalm 40:1-2). God the Father was looked upon corporately by ancient Israel as the great Emancipator from Egyptian bondage. Today every child of God can and should have a similar praise for God the Father who has saved them from the slavery of sin. It is solely through the mercies of God our Father that we are no longer wretched slaves to sin (Rom. 6:1-7).

3. God demonstrates his fatherhood to us furthermore as our constant protector. He preserves us from evil, both seen and unseen. He shields us from harm. He rescues us from danger. "God is our refuge and strength, a very present help in trouble" (Ps. 46:1). That is the role of any normal human father, who will even place himself at risk if necessary to protect those under his care. How much more is this true with our heavenly Father. The psalmist exults, "He who dwells in the secret place of the Most High shall abide under the shadow of the Almighty," and then he adds, "No evil shall befall you, nor shall any plague come near your dwelling" (Ps. 91:1, 10).

4. Our earthly fathers serve as providers of the needs of those under their care. To an even greater extend so is it also with our Heavenly Father. In the Sermon on the

Mount, Jesus talked at length about the loving provision of our Heavenly Father (Matt. 6:25-34). "Do not worry about your life, . . . If God so clothes the grass of the field, *will He* not much more *clothe* you? . . . But seek first the kingdom of God and His righteousness, and all these things shall be added to you. . . . Do not worry about tomorrow." In a normal family, our young children learn to trust us to provide for them. They have no need to worry. Neither should we.

5. Our Heavenly Father is also our guide. Life is uncertain. There are difficult choices to be made. Mistakes can be costly or even fatal. Job, even in the midst of the greatest trial imaginable, said, "He knows the way that I take; . . . My foot has held fast to His steps; I have kept His way and not turned aside (Job 23:10-11). Thankfully, there are no surprises for God. His word assures us, "The steps of a *good* man are ordered by the Lord, and He delights in his way. Though he fall, he shall not be utterly cast down; for the Lord upholds *him with* His hand" (Ps. 37:23-24).

6. Good fathers are also teachers. They instruct their children in many areas. They supervise their education. In a similar vein, our Heavenly Father is our loving instructor. This book, *Our Great God*, is part of a series entitled "Teach Me Your Paths." That title is drawn from a great prayer in Psalm 25. "Show me Your ways, O Lord; teach me Your paths. Lead me in Your truth and teach me" (Ps. 25:4-5). Our Heavenly Father loves to teach us, and as all normal children, we delight in learning.

7. The primary way our Heavenly Father instructs us is through the Bible. It is his written revelation to us. It serves to instruct us, but it also serves to discipline us, which is yet another characteristic of our Heavenly Father. He is our disciplinarian. In one of the best-known verses in Paul's writing he says about the revelation of our Heavenly Father, "All Scripture *is* given by inspiration of God, and *is* profitable for doctrine, for reproof, for correction, for instruction in righteousness" (2 Timothy 3:16). As we have seen before, the written revelation of God gives us good teaching ("doctrine"), but it also reproves and corrects us. Our Heavenly Father reproves and corrects us and does so primarily through his written word. That is why it is so important that we deeply cherish the Bible and dig into it with earnest attention on a daily basis.

8. Finally, let us rejoice that our Heavenly Father is both our counselor and our deliverer. Good fathers are good counselors, and good fathers always come to the rescue when they are needed. In the great revelation of the coming of the Messiah in Isaiah 9:6, we read that "His name will be called Wonderful, Counselor, Mighty God, Everlasting Father, Prince of Peace." Our Heavenly Father is our Counselor. And we can always count on him in the day of our greatest need. Paul said of our great Heavenly Father, "He has delivered us from the power of darkness and conveyed *us* into the kingdom of the Son of His love" (Col 1:13). Truly we serve a great God!

## Questions

1. Why is the teaching about the fatherhood of God not well understand within African Traditional Religion?

2. How does our creation and our salvation relate to God as a Heavenly Father?

3. What are some of the ways in which our Heavenly Father provides for us?

4. What is the primary way in which our Heavenly Father instructs us?

5. What are some of the ways in which our Heavenly Father surpasses the love, care and protection of our earthly fathers?

## Things to Think About

❖ *There is no other religion whose teachings about God can be compared with what the Bible reveals about the fatherhood of our Creator God.*

❖ *Even if we may have had a negative experience with our earthly father we can learn about the meaning of true fatherhood by drawing close to God the Father.*

96

# PART
# THREE

# GOD THE SON

We have taken time to understand the nature of our great God in the opening lessons of this study. We have delved into the truth of God as trinity: Father, Son and Holy Spirit. And we have also looked at what we can see and understand about God our Heavenly Father. We have continually also reminded ourselves that as finite humans we can never plumb the depths of the nature of an infinite God.

We have seen that the reality of God as a Heavenly Father is clearly shown through the scriptures. Through creation he is the Father of all of the human race. In a special way he was the Father of the nation Israel. And through salvation we can know him personally as our loving Father, so that when we pray we can with great meaning begin our praying with the words, "Our Father."

Now we come to a study of what we can learn from the scriptures about the Second Person of the Trinity, which is Jesus Christ, the Son of God. It is here that we come the closest to a personal revelation of God to man. The reason is obvious: God the Father sent his Son, Jesus Christ, to be incarnated in human flesh. John tells us in his gospel that "In the beginning was the Word, and the Word was with God, and the Word was God" (John 1:1). Then he tells us, "The Word became flesh and dwelt among us, and we beheld His glory" (v. 14). That was Jesus of Nazareth. That was the long-promised Messiah. It is the most incredible and wonderful revelation ever made by God the Father, of his own Son, Jesus Christ.

# OUR GREAT GOD

# JESUS CHRIST IS ETERNAL

### John 8:57-58; Colossians 1:17; Revelation 13:8; Hebrews 13:8

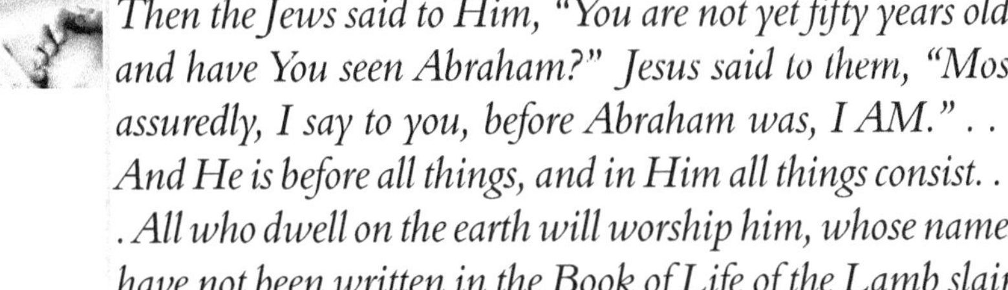

*Then the Jews said to Him, "You are not yet fifty years old, and have You seen Abraham?" Jesus said to them, "Most assuredly, I say to you, before Abraham was, I AM." . . . And He is before all things, and in Him all things consist. . . . All who dwell on the earth will worship him, whose names have not been written in the Book of Life of the Lamb slain from the foundation of the world. . . . Jesus Christ is the same yesterday, today, and forever.*

## Lesson Theme

There are a number of heretical Christian sects with false teachings about Jesus Christ, the Son of God. Examples can be found with both the Jehovah's Witnesses and the Church of Jesus Christ of Latter Day Saints (Mormons). These groups teach that Jesus was not eternal, that he is not truly God, but that he was created by God the Father. These are false teachings and should not be embraced by any true lover of the Bible. We will see in this lesson that there are multiple evidences within the scriptures that the

Jesus who was incarnated as a baby in Bethlehem and who lived and died as a man and who was later resurrected and ascended into heaven, was eternally part of the Godhead. Jesus Christ, the Son of God, has eternally existed and will live and reign forever with God the Father and God the Holy Spirit, as our one blessed Trinity.

## Introduction

In John 8 we see a dispute between Jesus and the Pharisees in which Jesus repeatedly defended himself in the face of their radical unbelief. It is was in this setting that Jesus made such strong statements about his identity with God the Father that his accusers took up stones to kill him as a blasphemer (v. 59). When he seemed to them to imply superiority over Abraham their ire was kindled. Jesus then said, "Before Abraham was, I AM" (v. 58). "I AM" was a direct reference to the personal name of God in the Old Testament, translated Yahweh, or Jehovah. Yahweh is the God who has always been, who is, and who always will be, therefore he is always the great "I AM." With this kind of statement, it was clear that Jesus was identifying himself as the Son of God who had eternally existed with God the Father and God the Holy Spirit. He is the eternal Son of God.

## Lesson

1. We have already seen that it is impossible for finite people to comprehend the depth of the Godhood. Though we may have some very basic understanding, the Trinity will forever remain a mystery to us. But

what we can be assured of is that God is not only omnipotent, omniscient and omnipresent, but he is also immutable, or unchangeable. In Malachi 3:6 God tells us, "For I *am* the Lord, I do not change." James 1:17 similarly says, "Every good gift and every perfect gift is from above, and comes down from the Father of lights, with whom there is no variation or shadow of turning."

**It is difficult for us to understand that Jesus, the Son of God, was part of the eternal Trinity that has always existed and will always exist.**

2. The doctrine of the eternal Sonship of Christ has been held by a majority of Christians throughout the centuries, even though there have been a minority of strong believers in the Trinity and in the full deity of Jesus Christ who have taught that the eternally-existing Christ became the Son at the point of his incarnation or some time thereafter. It is good for us, however, to remember the words of the Nicene Creed (325 AD)

about the nature of Christ: "We believe in one God, the Father, the Almighty, maker of heaven and earth, of all that is, seen and unseen We believe in one Lord, Jesus Christ, the only Son of God, eternally begotten of the Father, God from God, Light from Light, true God from true God, begotten, not make, of one Being with the Father. Through him all things were made. For us and for our salvation he came down from heaven: by the power of the Holy Spirit he became incarnate from the Virgin Mary and was made man."

3. There is good scriptural evidence that Jesus Christ was the eternal Son of God. For example, there are many Bible passages that tell us clearly that it was "the Son" who created all things (Col. 1:13-16; Heb. 1:2). This tells us that Jesus Christ was the Son of God long before the incarnation, at the time of creation.

4. We can also see numerous Bible passages that describe God the Father as sending the Son into the world to save sinners. Galatians 4:4, for example, says, "But when the fullness of the time had come, God sent forth His Son, born of a woman, born under the law." 1 John 4:10 says, "In this is love, not that we loved God, but that He loved us and sent His Son *to be* the propitiation for our sins." And how could we forget the most famous and often-quoted verse in the entire Bible: "For God so loved the world that He gave His only begotten Son, that whoever believes in Him should not perish but have everlasting life" (John 3:16)? It is clear from Galatians 4:4-6 that both the Son and the Holy Spirit were "sent forth" at a point in order to do the work of

God in this world. In both cases it is clear that the Son and the Holy Spirit were already part of the eternal Trinity that existed long before the creation of the world, and indeed forever.

5. Jesus Christ, who had eternally existed as part of the great Trinity, was "manifested" at the appointed time of the Father. John tells us that prior to the incarnation Jesus was eternally "in the bosom" of the Father (John 1:18), meaning that the incarnation was the revelation of the Son of God who had always existed.

6. One of the most direct statements about the eternal Sonship of Jesus Christ are the familiar words of Hebrews 13:8. "Jesus Christ *is* the same yesterday, today, and forever." This tells us that while Jesus took on human flesh at the time of the incarnation it did not in any way change his eternal nature. Jesus did not *become* the Son of God, because he always was the Son of God.

7. No doubt the strongest argument for the eternal Sonship of Christ is the very nature of the Trinity itself. God is an eternal Trinity. The relationship between the Father and the Son was an eternal relationship, even in the endless ages before the creation of the world and before the creation of Adam and Eve and their fall into sin. God the Father loved the Son long before there were lost people for whom he could send his Son as a worthy sacrifice for sin. And in fact, it is a measure of the incomprehensible love of God that he was willing

to send his one and only Son to die in our place. Truly we serve a great God!

## Questions

1. What do the Jehovah's Witnesses and the Mormons have in common about their belief concerning Jesus Christ?

2. Explain what Jesus meant when he told the Pharisees, "Before Abraham was, I AM"?

3. What are some of the scriptural evidences we have seen in this lesson that teach the eternal Sonship of Jesus Christ?

4. Explain the meaning of Hebrews 13:8, "Jesus Christ is the same yesterday, today, and forever."

5. How does the existence of the Trinity help establish the truth of the eternal Sonship of Jesus Christ?

## Things to Think About

❖ *One of the surest ways to discover the false teachings of the Christian cults is to examine their attempts to diminish the Person and ministry of Jesus Christ.*

❖ *We must always seek to consciously praise and worship God as he is: an eternal Trinity of Father, Son and Holy Spirit.*

# THE PROPHETIC PREPARATION FOR JESUS

### Genesis 3:15; Isaiah 9:6; Micah 5:2; Malachi 3:1

*And I will put enmity between you and the woman, and between your seed and her Seed; He shall bruise your head, and you shall bruise His heel." ...For unto us a Child is born, unto us a Son is given; and the government will be upon His shoulder. And His name will be called Wonderful, Counselor, Mighty God, Everlasting Father, Prince of Peace... "But you, Bethlehem Ephrathah, though you are little among the thousands of Judah, yet out of you shall come forth to Me the One to be Ruler in Israel, Whose goings forth are from of old, from everlasting." ..."Behold, I send My messenger, and he will prepare the way before Me. And the Lord, whom you seek, will suddenly come to His temple, even the Messenger of the covenant, in whom you delight. Behold, He is coming," says the Lord of hosts.*

## Lesson Theme

We have seen how important the revelation of the Trinity is within the Bible. Though we do not see its complete revelation until the pages of the New Testament we know that even in the Old Testament we can see the working of God the Son and God the Holy Spirit. Then as we open the four gospels in the New Testament we see the stunning revelation of the incarnation, which is Jesus Christ, the Son of God, born in Bethlehem, nurtured in Nazareth, and brought into full ministry in Galilee, Judea and beyond. What we are going to see in this lesson is that the coming of this great Messiah into the world was not something that came unannounced. To the contrary, it had been predicted in various details for hundreds of years before. Right from the proclamation of God in the Garden of Eden that the seed of Eve would strike the head of the serpent we have the foretelling of the work of Jesus Christ as the incarnate Redeemer.

## Introduction

There are scores of prophecies from the pages of the Old Testament that pointed God's people forward to the coming of Jesus Christ as Messiah. In this lesson we can only mention some of them. What we see is a clear picture of the intentions of God the Father. Knowing that human beings whom he had created had fallen away into sin and rebellion, God did not resign them to a hopeless fate of eternal damnation. He had established an eternal decree that "The soul who sins shall die" (Ezek. 18:20, cf. Rom. 6:23, "The wages of sin is death"). Our loving Heavenly Father knew that the only remedy was the sending of his one and only eternal Son, to live and die on behalf of an entire sinful race. So, generation after generation throughout the Old Testament the prophetic words rang out. "Messiah is coming!" Let us see in this lesson some of those ringing prophesies.

## Lesson

1. When we look at the first three chapters in the Book of Genesis it becomes clear that Yahweh, the Creator God, is intent on bringing salvation to fallen humanity. The creation of Adam and Eve in the image of God is the setting of the stage. God created us in his image for the sole purpose of eternal fellowship with himself, on the basis of shared character. In order for that to be true it was necessary for us to be endowed with the gift of free choice, so that with such freedom we could experience a loving relationship never knowable by brute beasts. Yet our first parents fell into sin and suddenly a great gulf was opened between God and humanity. However, it was at that point that God made the first pronouncement of a plan of salvation. In order for humanity to be brought back into fellowship with God it would be necessary for a decisive blow to be made against the serpent, in the form of a Messiah who could destroy the works of Satan and bring salvation to all humanity. That is why in Genesis 3:15 we have the first triumphant note announcing God's solution. God said, "I will put enmity between you and the woman, and between your seed and her Seed; He shall bruise your head, and you shall bruise His heel."

**The prophecy of Simeon over the baby Jesus at the time of his circumcision was the last of a long line of prophesies concerning the coming Messiah.**

2. We refer to the Old Testament promises and prophecies of the coming of Jesus Christ as *messianic*. A messianic promise is a promise of the eventual coming of the Messiah. The word *Messiah* is from the Hebrew *Mashiach*, meaning "anointed one." It has a similar meaning as the Greek word *Christ*. To refer to Jesus of Nazareth as "Jesus Christ," therefore, is to express belief that Jesus of Nazareth is the long-prophesied Messiah of the Old Testament. He is from the royal line of David, who was the greatest anointed king of Israel. We also discover that it was through Jesus Christ eventually that the royal line of David was established for all ages (Ps. 132:10-11).

3. It has been suggested by some scholars that there are more than 300 messianic prophecies in the Old Testament, all pointing eventually to Jesus. More than forty times in the New Testament we are told that certain things that happened in the life of Jesus occurred "so that the scripture would be fulfilled" (e.g., Mat. 26:54; John 19:36). The tracing of these references leaves us with a rich understanding that Jesus, the Son of God, was foreseen and foretold for hundreds of years before he was born in Bethlehem.

4. We can see throughout the Old Testament that Jesus Christ, the Messiah, is referred to with a variety of titles. In the prophecies of Isaiah, for example, the Messiah is referred to as the "Servant of the Lord." The most well-known such prophesy is Isaiah 53, where we see the prophesy of a "Suffering Servant," which was so powerfully descriptive of the sacrifice eventually made by Jesus Christ.  Other prophecies refer to the Messiah as the "Star" of Judah (Num. 24:17). Isaiah 11:1 depicts the Messiah as a "Branch" bearing bountiful fruit. Even more common are many depictions of the Messiah as a coming King who will rule in righteousness and confound the nations (Is. 9:6; Jer. 23:5; Zech. 9:9).

5. The New Testament book that gives us the clearest reflection on the fulfillment of Old Testament messianic prophecies is Matthew's gospel. This gospel was obviously written to Jewish readers. In deference to the Jewish custom of avoiding the pronouncing of the name of God, for example, Matthew refers to the "kingdom of God" as the "kingdom of heaven," which

is peculiar to his own gospel. Matthew's gospel is filled with many references to fulfilled prophecies about the Messiah. His virgin birth is a fulfillment of Isaiah 7:14, for example (cf. Mat. 1:18-23). His flight to Egypt was a fulfillment of Hosea 11:1 (cf. Mat. 2:15). His triumphal entry into Jerusalem on Palm Sunday fulfilled Zechariah 9:9 (cf. Mat. 21:1-5). Many more examples could be given.

6. We know also that there are certain types and shadows in the Old Testament that point to the coming of the Messiah. The most apparent one involves the sacrificial system established in the tabernacle and temple. There it was that Yahweh instructed Israel to offering regular sacrifices of various kinds and to drill deep into their hearts the understanding that "it is the blood that makes atonement for the soul" (Lev. 17:11). In the Book of Hebrews, we see that same repeated refrain ("without shedding of blood there is no remission" [9:22]). There also it is clearly revealed that it is Jesus himself who becomes our great High Priest, offering up an eternal sacrifice that far surpassed the temporary annual sacrifice offered by the Old Testament High Priest (Heb. 9:23-28).

7. We can also point to Old Testament characters whose lives and actions foreshadowed and at least indirectly pointed to a coming future Messiah. The life of Joseph is one example. Joseph's rejection by his family foreshadows Jesus' rejection, and his eventual exaltation to the highest possible position looks forward to the elevation of Jesus Christ to the right

hand of the Father (Eph. 1:15-23). Likewise, we can see the example of Boaz in the Book of Ruth, who exemplified Jesus Christ as our great Kinsman Redeemer.

8.  Messianic prophecies are found in every part of the Old Testament, including the Law, the Prophets and the Writings. This is exactly what Jesus told the two discouraged disciples on the road to Emmaus. As recorded by Luke, Jesus said, "These *are* the words which I spoke to you while I was still with you, that all things must be fulfilled which were written in the Law of Moses and *the* Prophets and *the* Psalms concerning Me" (Luke 24:44). What Jesus was telling them was that God had faithfully promised the coming of Jesus Christ, the Son of God, as the great Messiah. Therefore, it was absolutely essential that it all should be fulfilled ("all things *must* be fulfilled"). We can only stand back in awe once again and say, "What a great God we serve!"

## Questions

1.  Why do you think it is so important that the first prophecy about the coming Messiah is found so near the beginning of Genesis, in Genesis 3:15?

2.  What does the word "Messiah" mean, and what do we mean by a messianic prophecy?

3.  What are some of the titles by which the prophesied Messiah is called in the Old Testament?

4. What is peculiar about the gospel of Matthew with respect to the messianic prophecies?

5. Who are some of the characters in the Old Testament whose lives foreshadowed that of Jesus?

## Things to Think About

❖ *There is enough evidence within the Old Testament alone for one to become convinced of the truth of Jesus Christ as the Son of God.*

❖ *One of the greatest proofs of the infallibility and divine inspiration of the Bible is the close agreement between the picture of the Messiah in both the Old Testament and the New Testament*

# THE MIRACLE OF THE INCARNATION

Isaiah 7:14; Luke 1:31, 35; Matthew 1:23; John 1:14

*And behold, you will conceive in your womb and bring forth a Son, and shall call His name Jesus. . . . And the angel answered and said to her, "The Holy Spirit will come upon you, and the power of the Highest will overshadow you; therefore, also, that Holy One who is to be born will be called the Son of God. . . . "Behold, the virgin shall be with child, and bear a Son, and they shall call His name Immanuel," which is translated, "God with us." . . . And the Word became flesh and dwelt among us, and we beheld His glory, the glory as of the only begotten of the Father, full of grace and truth.*

**Lesson Theme**

Our theme in this lesson is to show from the word of God that our Lord and Savior, Jesus Christ, was conceived of the Holy Spirit, born of the virgin Mary, and was born without original sin or the sin nature. We refer to this great event as the miracle of the incarnation. The word incarnation means literally "being made flesh," which is from the Latin translation of John 1:14. "The Word became flesh and dwelt among us." Jesus was the eternal Word who was present with the Father from endless past ages, but who at the "fullness of time" (Gal. 4:4-7) was revealed in true human flesh in a small town near Jerusalem.

## Introduction

In the last lesson we learned that Jesus Christ is the pre-existent Son of God who was boldly and repeatedly prophesied about in the Old Testament. We know that he existed throughout the eternal ages before the incarnation. In the Christmas story that we gladly repeat every year, we learn how Jesus became a man. In the word of Paul, he took upon himself the form and likeness of man (Phil. 2:5-8). John O. Walvoord has said that "The incarnation of the Lord Jesus Christ is the central fact of Christianity. Upon it the whole superstructure of Christian theology depends." In other words, our eternal salvation is closely linked with this doctrine. We can confidently say that if Jesus Christ was not born of a virgin, after being conceived by the Holy Spirit, then he could not have been the mediator between God and sinful man and we would all be lost without hope. But we thank our heavenly Father who has not hidden from us the truth about how Christ was born. He was virgin born, and he was also born free from sin. The mystery of the virgin birth is a glorious truth to be believed, adored and accepted by all Christians.

## Lesson

1. The Bible clearly teaches that Jesus Christ, the promised Messiah of the Old Testament, was born of a virgin (Is. 7:14; Mat. 1:23). As we know, a virgin is a woman who has not known a man sexually. According to the holy word of God, Mary remained a virgin until after the birth of Jesus, and until she and Joseph lived together as husband and wife. Matthew 1:18 and Luke 2:4-7 make these matters very clear. Through a mystery that we cannot understand, Mary was able to conceive through the power of the Holy Spirit and not from Joseph or any other man (John 1:13). Therefore, we know that the birth of Jesus Christ was the result of the activity of the Holy Spirit as the creative power of God. The virgin conception of our Lord is both a great mystery and a great miracle.

**The miracle of the incarnation is a necessary part of the foundation of our redemption.**

2. In order to be the Savior of all mankind, Jesus had to be not only divine, and virgin-born, but he had to also be truly human. This means he had to become a literal, physical descendent of Adam and Eve, which is the common mark of all of humanity. There are many evidences in the gospels that Jesus was truly human. He needed sleep (Luke 8:23). He ate food (Mat. 4:2; 21:18). He perspired and bled (Luke 22:43-44; John 19:34). He even referred to himself as a man, as we see in John 8:40. He was truly human, born of the "seed of David according to the flesh" (Rom. 1:3).

3. It is also important to acknowledge that for Jesus Christ to become the Savior of all mankind it was necessary for him to shed his blood on our behalf (Heb. 9:22). Yet such shedding of blood had to be on the part of someone who had a flesh and blood body like ours. This was the heart of the plan of the Heavenly Father for the incarnation. Hebrews 10:5 says, "Therefore, when He came into the world, He said: 'Sacrifice and offering You did not desire, but a body You have prepared for Me." If there had been no incarnation there could never have been an eternal sacrifice for our sins, and we would have been consigned to eternal doom.

4. It is a fundamental tenet of our Christian faith that Jesus was both fully God and fully man. This is a difficult truth for us to comprehend, yet it is a solid and undeniable Bible doctrine. Some even in modern times have rejected the belief that Jesus was fully God (the ancient Ebionites and modern Mormons). Others,

such as the ancient Docetics, claimed that Jesus was fully God but only *appeared* to be a human being. Paul explained why it is so important for us to embrace both the full deity and the full humanity of Jesus: "But when the fullness of the time had come, God sent forth His Son, born of a woman, born under the law, to redeem those who were under the law, that we might receive the adoption as sons" (Gal. 4:4).

5.  Because Jesus was truly human he was and is able to relate to us in a way that could never happen on the part of angels, for example. The writer to the Hebrews says that Jesus sympathizes with our weaknesses and was tempted in every way just as we are (Heb. 4:15). Jesus was persecuted. He was despised and rejected. He suffered immense physical pain and underwent lingering torture and died a cruel and undeserved death. Because of that, he is able to bring courage and hope to those in similar circumstances.

6.  Romans 8:3-4 uses an interesting expression regarding the incarnation. "For what the law could not do in that it was weak through the flesh, God *did* by sending His own Son <u>in the likeness of sinful flesh</u>, on account of sin: He condemned sin in the flesh, that the righteous requirement of the law might be fulfilled in us who do not walk according to the flesh but according to the Spirit." When we speak of "sinful flesh" we refer to the fact that all of us inherit the fallen nature of mankind because of the original sin of Adam and Eve. However, we know that while Jesus was fully man, and truly "of

the seed of David according to the flesh," he was miraculously born without sin.

7. The Christian Church has always believed the importance of proclaiming both the deity and the humanity of Jesus Christ. Paul says, "If you confess with your mouth the Lord Jesus and believe in your heart that God has raised Him from the dead, you will be saved" (Rom 10:9), meaning that belief in Jesus as divine is necessary to our salvation. On the other hand, John said, "By this you know the Spirit of God: Every spirit that confesses that Jesus Christ has come in the flesh is of God" (1 John 4:2). John equally warns that to deny the true human nature of Jesus is a doctrine of antichrist. "For many deceivers have gone out into the world who do not confess Jesus Christ *as* coming in the flesh. This is a deceiver and an antichrist" (2 John 1:7). The eternal Son of God took on human flesh at a point, yet never at any time did he cease to be God. He was not half-God and half-human. He is the only eternally divine Person who has both divine and human natures.

8. We have cited before the timely and important reminder of Hebrews 13:8, which says, "Jesus Christ is the same yesterday, today and forever." What that tells us is that Jesus Christ was the glorious Son of God from all eternity past and that he did not cease to be God at the incarnation. He did not become half-God and half-man. Jesus was and is and shall forever be both God and man. Truly we serve a great God!

## Questions

1. What are some of the evidences within the gospels that Jesus was truly human?

2. Why was the incarnation so necessary for the sake of our salvation?

3. What did Paul mean by saying that Jesus was "in the likeness of sinful flesh" (Rom. 8:3-4)?

4. Explain why both the deity and humanity of Jesus are necessary and biblical truths.

5. What do we mean when we say that "Jesus Christ is the same yesterday, today and forever" (Heb. 13:8)?

## Things to Think About

❖ *Those who deny the virgin birth of Jesus are often the same ones who do not accept the miracle of the incarnation and do not believe that Jesus is the true and only fully divine and fully human Savior.*

❖ *It is because of the incarnation that we can come boldly to the throne of grace, knowing that Jesus is our Elder Brother even now interceding for us at the right hand of the Father.*

# OUR GREAT GOD

# THE EARTHLY MINISTRY OF JESUS

Galatians 4:4-5; Luke 3:21-23; Matthew 4:23-25; 1 Peter 2:21-24

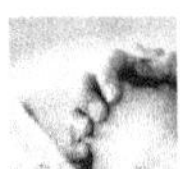

*But when the fullness of the time had come, God sent forth His Son, born of a woman, born under the law, to redeem those who were under the law, that we might receive the adoption as sons. . . . When all the people were baptized, it came to pass that Jesus also was baptized; and while He prayed, the heaven was opened. And the Holy Spirit descended in bodily form like a dove upon Him, and a voice came from heaven which said, "You are My beloved Son; in You I am well pleased." Now Jesus Himself began His ministry at about thirty years of age. . . . And Jesus went about all Galilee, teaching in their synagogues, preaching the gospel of the kingdom, and healing all kinds of sickness and all kinds of disease among the people. Then His fame went throughout all Syria; and they brought to Him all sick people who were afflicted with various diseases and torments, and those who were demon-possessed, epileptics, and paralytics; and He healed them. Great multitudes followed Him from Galilee, and from Decapolis, Jerusalem, Judea, and beyond the Jordan. . . . Christ also suffered for us,*

> *leaving us an example, that you should follow His steps:*
> *'Who committed no sin, nor was deceit found in His*
> *mouth'; who, when He was reviled, did not revile in return;*
> *when He suffered, He did not threaten, but committed*
> *Himself to Him who judges righteously; who Himself bore*
> *our sins in His own body on the tree.*

## Lesson Theme

Up to this point we have been looking at the big picture of our salvation and how it is related to the coming of Jesus Christ in human flesh and his eventual self-sacrifice for the sins of the whole world. Jesus was God-come-in-the-flesh. He was the perfect sacrifice that opened the door of salvation to all of humanity. Yet that is not the entire story about Jesus of Nazareth. Jesus was born as a baby in Bethlehem, and he lived on this earth for more than thirty years. In the words of Peter, through his perfect life he was "leaving us an example," so that we could follow his steps (1 Pet. 2:21). This enables us to see that it is not only the death and resurrection of Jesus that are important but also the life that he lived. In this lesson we will look at why and how the ministry of Jesus of Nazareth is important to us even today.

## Introduction

One of the blessings we enjoy today is that we have not just one account of the life and ministry of Jesus, but four. In fact, we have evidences of the life and reputation of Jesus also in the Book of Acts and indirectly in several other New Testament letters, and even from a few sources outside of the New Testament. Though Jesus lived 2,000 years ago we have a rich record of his deeds and teachings and certainly far more than any other people living in the ancient world during the First Century. It is important for us to understand why this record is important to us even today.

## Lesson

1. There are various opinions on the length of Jesus' ministry, and the reason is that in reading the four gospels we do not get precise dates as we have come to expect in the writing of history in modern times. However, we know from a close examination that there are four different Passover events mentioned in the gospels, including the Passover during which Jesus was arrested and crucified. Passover was the greatest event on the annual Jewish calendar and was always celebrated by Jesus and his disciples. We also know that his baptism and launching of his public ministry began before the first Passover that is mentioned, so therefore most Bible scholars are of the opinion that the public ministry of Jesus lasted for about three and a half years. A broad overview of those three years is that the first year could be called the Year of Obscurity (while Jesus was still largely unknown both in Galilee and Judea), the Year of Popularity (in which large crowds began to follow him at times), and the Year of Opposition (when gathering clouds of opposition eventually led to his arrest, crucifixion and death).

**Jesus spent more of his ministry teaching and preaching to small groups, and especially to his twelve disciples.**

2.  Another way to examine Jesus' ministry is through the lens of geography. After the opening events of his baptism and his temptation in the wilderness we see his earliest ministry in Judea, which is then followed by his early teachings in his native Galilee. Much of his ministry then continued in Galilee, where his home base was not his boyhood home in Nazareth but the seaside town of Capernaum, near the southern end of the Sea of Galilee. This was followed by his return for a period of ministry in Judea, and then later his travel across the Jordan to the northeast in what is referred to as his Perean ministry. Finally, he concluded his ministry during the Passion Week in Jerusalem, and then his resurrection and ascension to heaven.

3.  There are few people who have made such an enormous impact in such a short period of time as did Jesus of Nazareth. In a period of three short years this

man Jesus changed the entire course of history. How did he do it? What exactly was it that made his ministry so effective as to change the world of his own day and still have lasting and strong impact today after 2,000 years? What was the nature of his teaching that so dramatically changed the entire world?

4. One of the first things that strikes us about Jesus' teaching is its *simplicity*. He was quiet. He was gentle. He was able to communicate to the lowest of the low, as well as to kings and rulers, before whom he was meek and lowly. Jesus never wrote a book. He never built a building, raised a monument or marshaled an army. He totally defied the expectations of his followers, who wanted a flamboyant, loud and decorated Messiah. Such people had risen from time to time, and fairly quickly were defeated. But Jesus was not that way. Matthew said, *"He will not quarrel or cry out; no one will hear His voice in the streets. A bruised reed He will not break, and a smoldering wick He will not snuff out"* (Matthew 12:20, quoting Isaiah 42:3).

5. Jesus was uniquely able to reach out to *everyone* in his ministry, and not to just a few. The result is that the Christian message even today has broad international, interracial, intercultural and interreligious appeal. Though he was born as a Jew, in his ministry Jesus reached out to Samaritans, Greeks, young and old, rich and poor, and the educated and uneducated. Today Christianity remains the most universal of messages in the world, totally unlike other world religions that are culturally and geographically bound.

6. Jesus' ministry was also marked by *unusual authority* that could not be mistaken. At the close of the Sermon on the Mount, as recorded by Matthew, it says that *"the people were astonished at His teaching, or He taught them as one having authority, and not as the scribes"* (Matthew 7:28b-29). The scribes got their authority from their ability to quote from all the ancient Jewish authorities, but Jesus spoke by his own authority, and was able to say boldly, *"All authority is given unto Me in heaven and on earth"* (Matthew 28:18). Who but Jesus Christ could talk like that and command the respect of his listeners and then inspire them to go to the ends of the earth to proclaim it?

7. Jesus ministry was also distinct because it was accompanied by *awesome power*. His words were backed up by divine power. He performed not just one or two miracles, but hundreds. When John the Baptist was thrown into prison and was tempted to doubt Jesus, he told two of his disciples, *"Go back and report to John what you hear and see: The blind receive sight, the lame walk, those who have leprosy are cured, the deaf hear, the dead are raised, and the good news is preaching to the poor"* (Mat. 11:4-5).

8. Jesus' ministry was characterized by an unusually positive attitude toward both women and children. Today such an attitude is expected and followed throughout much of the world and it is easy to forget that it was Jesus himself who upset the pattern of neglect and even abuse of women and children. Wherever Christianity has spread it has encouraged equal treatment of men and women, and due attention

to children. All four gospel writers highlight Jesus' interaction with women. He pointed out the poor widow who gave her offering (Mark 12:41), and he was especially close to women such as Mary and Martha (John 11). He refused to condemn the woman taken in adultery (John 8:1-11) and showed pity for the Phoenician woman by healing her daughter (Mat. 15:21-28), etc.

9. Finally, we note that Jesus not only uttered truth, but he also made amazing claims about himself, as no other teacher before or after could have done. He said things about himself that no other person would dare say. He boldly claimed to be the Messiah. *"The woman said, 'I know that Messiah (called Christ) is coming. When He comes, He will explain everything to us.' Then Jesus declared, 'I who speak to you am He'"* (John 4:25-26). Luke 22:70 records Jesus' claim that he was God himself: *"They all asked, 'Are you then the Son of God?' He replied, 'You are right in saying I am.'"* Truly no man ever spoke as this man. He is Jesus. He is the Son of God. He is the Messiah. We do well to worship him all the days of our life!

## Questions

1. Why do we believe the public ministry of Jesus lasted for three-and-one-half years?

2. What do we mean when we say that we can examine Jesus' ministry through the lens of geography?

3. Explain how the ministry of Jesus was simple and why it nevertheless had some enormous impact.

4. How was the authority of Jesus expressed during his ministry, and what were the signs of power that accompanied it?

5. What was unique about the attitude of Jesus toward women and children, and how did he display it?

## Things to Think About

❖ *No other three-year period in the entire history of the world was more important and more world changing than the three years of Jesus' ministry.*

❖ *Jesus Christ of Nazareth was both the gentlest and the most powerful teacher ever to command the attention of his disciples.*

# THE PASSION OF JESUS

### Isaiah 53:3-5; Hebrews 5:7-8; 1 Peter 4:13

*He is despised and rejected by men, a Man of sorrows and acquainted with grief. And we hid, as it were, our faces from Him; He was despised, and we did not esteem Him. Surely He has borne our griefs and carried our sorrows; yet we esteemed Him stricken, smitten by God, and afflicted. But He was wounded for our transgressions, He was bruised for our iniquities; the chastisement for our peace was upon Him, and by His stripes we are healed. . . . who, in the days of His flesh, when He had offered up prayers and supplications, with vehement cries and tears to Him who was able to save Him from death, and was heard because of His godly fear, though He was a Son, yet He learned obedience by the things which He suffered. . . . but rejoice to the extent that you partake of Christ's sufferings, that when His glory is revealed, you may also be glad with exceeding joy.*

## Lesson Theme

When we talk about the passion of Christ we refer to the time starting with his agonizing prayer in the Garden of Gethsemane until his death by crucifixion the following day. We sometimes refer to the entire week leading up to the resurrection of Jesus on Easter Sunday as Passion Week. All four of the gospels devote a major portion of their writing to this most important week in the history of the world. The passion of Jesus Christ is recorded in Matthew 26:36-27:56, Mark 14:32-15:41, Luke 22:39-23:49 and John 18:1-19:37. These events have been most vividly portrayed in recent years by Mel Gibson's film, *The Passion of the Christ*. There are few people who desire to view that film a second time, since it so vividly depicts the terrible agonies undertaken by Jesus on behalf of lost humanity.

## Introduction

The word *passion* means simply suffering. Jesus Christ suffered for all of us, as had long been predicted by the prophets. Just as Isaiah said, he was "wounded for our transgressions" and received bruises, chastisement and stripes to bring about our own healing (Is. 53:3-5). What is clear also is that once Jesus had suffered on the cross for our redemption this became the focal point of the preaching of the Early Church. It is very true that they celebrated the resurrection, but they also knew that the significance of the resurrection was that it affirmed the purpose of Jesus' sacrificial death and testified to the fact that the Heavenly Father had accepted that sin offering much as the sin offering of the ancient High Priest had been accepted in earlier years. Paul expressed his own feelings about it when he said, "For I determined not to know anything among you except Jesus Christ and Him crucified" (1 Cor. 2:2). It is because of the suffering of Jesus that you and I are brought into reconciliation with God.

## Lesson

1.  There were people in the First Century who denied that Jesus was truly human and that he therefore had a human body like our own. These Docetics, as they were called, were influenced by Greek philosophy to believe that since human flesh is sinful Jesus only *appeared* to be human. Therefore, he could not have suffered the agonies that seem to be described in the gospels. But the Bible lets us know very plainly that Jesus truly suffered and died for us. We see him in the Garden of Gethsemane sweating as if it were great drops of blood and appealing to his Heavenly Father to allow him to escape his impending suffering. Luke 22:44 says, "And being in agony, He prayed more earnestly. Then His sweat became like great drops of blood falling down to the ground." Jesus's intense suffering had been predicted hundreds of years earlier by Isaiah, who described him as "stricken," "afflicted," "pierced," "crushed," "wounded," "oppressed," etc. It is difficult for us to comprehend the extent of Jesus' suffering, and it was unquestionably real and not imaginary.

**The passion or suffering of Jesus was a necessary part of our eternal redemption. Isaiah said, "It pleased the Lord to bruise him" (Is. 53:10).**

2. We know that before Jesus was finally taken to the cross he had to undergo the terrible scourging that was so common among the Romans. The Apostle Paul experienced that type of punishment himself, though from the Jews, and also as an innocent man. He says in 2 Corinthians 11:24, "From the Jews five times I received forty stripes minus one." We have no idea how many stripes Jesus received, but we do know that Pontius Pilate order him to be flogged, though not so as to kill him (Mat. 27:26). These were the very "stripes" Isaiah had prophesied earlier. What appears most alarming to all of this is that many of these people who were meting out such hatred and injustice against Jesus must have known that he was an innocent man. The depth of wickedness within the human heart is clearly revealed,

and all the more when we realize that the victim of their cruelty was the incarnate Son of God.

3.  What was happening here was a most amazing, eternal and glorious transaction. We can remember that Isaiah said, "By His stripes we are healed," and "The LORD has laid on Him the iniquity of us all" (Is. 53:5-6). This is surely difficult to comprehend. Jesus was innocent, yet he was also the sacrificial Lamb of God. He told his disciples earlier, "I lay down My life for the sheep" (John 10:15). Now he willingly does it, and through his stripes we find eternal healing. Peter refers to Jesus as the one who, "Bore our sins in His own body on the tree, that we, having died to sins, might live for righteousness, by whose stripes you were healed" (1 Pet. 2:24). That healing is far more than physical healing. It means primarily that the suffering of Christ enables us to be forever free from the slavery of sin and to dwell in eternal fellowship with our great God, seated with Jesus Christ at the right hand of the Father (Eph. 2:6).

4.  In Jerusalem during Passion Week, Jesus was not only scourged, but he journeyed from Pilate's judgement hall to Calvary's hill along what has been called the Via Dolorosa, of the "Way of Pain." After Pilate's judgment Jesus was flogged, mocked, spit upon and then forced to carry his own cross through the street of Jerusalem. Today one can go to the Old City of Jerusalem and see fourteen "stations of the cross" where according to Church tradition various incidents in that painful journey took place. We cannot be sure of many of the

alleged details, but we know that his suffering was real, and that the greatest pain was his bearing of the sins of the whole world on his shoulders.

5. It is very legitimate for us to ask why all of this suffering on the part of Jesus was necessary. What we can see from the words of Jesus himself was that he understood that his suffering was not simply the result of cruelty or hatred on the part of either the Jews or the Romans. Rather, as he had told his disciples much earlier, he understood that "The Son of Man <u>must</u> suffer many things and be rejected by the elders and chief priests and scribes, and be killed, and be raised the third day" (Luke 9:22). The suffering of Jesus Christ was at the core of God's eternal plan for the redemption of lost sinners.

6. What this further shows us is that God does not take the issue of sin lightly. Both in the Old Testament and the New Testament the proclamation of scripture is that "The soul who sins shall die" (Ezek. 18:20), and "The wages of sin is death" (Rom. 6:23). We must never forget that sin is a dreadful killer. God's wrath will forever be leveled against sin, which at its core is rebellion. The fact that God sent his one and only Son to suffer the worst that humanity could throw against him is an eternal measure of how seriously God considers the issue of sin and the lengths to which he was willing to go to redeem us from its curse.

7. There is a verse in Paul's writings concerning the suffering of Christ that has raised questions over the years. In 1 Colossians 1:24 Paul says, "I now rejoice in

my sufferings for you, and fill up in my flesh what is lacking in the afflictions of Christ, for the sake of His body, which is the church." What does Paul mean by something that is "lacking in the afflictions of Christ"? Paul is not saying here that there was something inadequate about the suffering of Christ. Rather, he is referring to his own suffering. The New Living Translation gives us a clearer understanding: "I am glad when I suffer for you in my body, for I am participating in the sufferings of Christ that continue for his body, the church." In other words, Paul understood that through his own sufferings he was better able to relate to and conform to the very spirit of submission to the Father that allowed Jesus to go to the cross on our behalf.

8. The question all of us can ask at this point is about our own response to the enormous sufferings of Christ. What should be our response?  Surely, we must bow in worship and gratitude. We must also be willing to take up our own cross and follow Christ (Luke 9:23). We can also say with the writer to the Hebrews, "Let us run with endurance the race God has set before us. We do this by keeping our eyes on Jesus, the champion who initiates and perfects our faith. Because of the joy awaiting him, he endured the cross, disregarding its shame. Now he is seated in the place of honor beside God's throne" (Heb. 12:1-3). Surely, we serve a great God. Hallelujah!

## Questions

1.  What do we mean by the passion of Jesus?

2.  Who were the Docetics of the First Century, and what did they believe about the suffering of Jesus?

3.  What were the stripes that Jesus received, and what did Isaiah mean by writing, "by his stripes we are healed"?

4.  What is the Via Dolorosa in Jerusalem?

5.  Why was the suffering of Jesus necessary?

## Things to Think About

❖ *The ignominy and shame of the suffering and death of Jesus would never have been a fabrication of a false religion. Its very shame is an indirect proof of its truth.*

❖ *The wounds of Christ are his greatest proof of his love toward us.*

# THE RESURRECTION OF JESUS

## Mark 8:31; Romans 4:23-25; 1 Corinthians 15:3-4

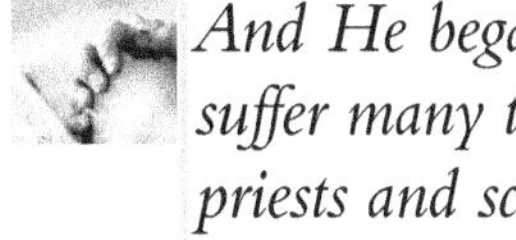

*And He began to teach them that the Son of Man must suffer many things, and be rejected by the elders and chief priests and scribes, and be killed, and after three days rise again. . . . Now it was not written for his sake alone that it was imputed to him, but also for us. It shall be imputed to us who believe in Him who raised up Jesus our Lord from the dead, who was delivered up because of our offenses, and was raised because of our justification. . . . For I delivered to you first of all that which I also received: that Christ died for our sins according to the Scriptures, and that He was buried, and that He rose again the third day according to the Scriptures,*

## Lesson Theme

The happenings that were packed into the week starting with the triumphal entry of Jesus into Jerusalem on Palm Sunday make up the absolutely most important week in the history of the world. Every event in that week is etched into our collective memories and together they are a divine drama not of fiction but of eternal reality. Jesus Christ was at the center stage. He had been incarnated more than thirty years earlier and was now at the conclusion of a three-year public ministry. Jesus' close disciples and followers were there, as well as the curious multitudes and his bitter enemies among the Jewish elite. As his enemies rushed him to judgement, condemnation and crucifixion it all seemed to end on Friday with a note of finality and defeat. But then Sunday came. With one mighty igniting of divine energy Jesus burst forth from the shackles of death and became not just Jesus of Nazareth, but the Risen Lord and Savior, and the incarnate Son of God come back to life. Hallelujah! Christ is risen!

## Introduction

Even if his disciples did not truly comprehend it, Jesus had more than once foretold his resurrection on the third day. He had even rebuked Peter for not accepting that revelation when Jesus and his disciples had crossed over the Jordan to Caesarea Philippi the year before. "From then on Jesus began to tell his disciples plainly that it was necessary for him to go to Jerusalem, and that he would suffer many terrible things at the hands of the elders, the leading priests, and the teachers of religious law. He would be killed, but <u>on the third day he would be raised from the dead</u>" (Mat. 16:21). Peter certainly heard the word "killed," but apparently "raised from the dead" did not register well on his brain. The result was that he resisted Jesus' statement ("Heaven forbid" [v. 22]), resulting in the sharpest rebuke Jesus ever gave to any of his disciples: "Get away from me, Satan!" (v. 23). Jesus knew he would die, but he knew also that he would completely and forever defeat death and vindicate his eternal sacrifice for sin through his bodily resurrection. That is what we want to look into in this lesson.

## Lesson

1. It should not be a surprise to anyone that the resurrection of Jesus is denied by some people. It would be difficult to deny the supernatural reality of Jesus if in fact he did what no other person in the history of the world has ever done by dying such a horrific death and then walking free and healthy from the tomb three days later. But that is exactly what happened, and there are a number of proofs that substantiate this most central of Christian teaching. Paul said bluntly, "If Christ has not been raised, then all our preaching is useless, and your faith is useless" (1 Cor. 15:14). In this lesson we will see that there are strong reasons why the resurrection of Jesus is an established fact of history. Even more importantly, we will see why the resurrection became a central theme of the Early Church and what it means for our teaching of salvation.

**The resurrection of Jesus is the focal point of all of human history.  Without it our faith is meaningless. With it, we have eternal salvation.**

2.  One measure of the importance of the resurrection of Jesus is that Paul devoted the entirety of the longest chapter in his epistles to this topic: 1 Corinthians 15. In that chapter he started by pointing out the place of the resurrection among the fundamental Christian beliefs about Jesus: that he died for our sins, that he was buried, that he rose again, and that he was seen by a host of witnesses thereafter. He also explained at length the meaning of the resurrection as a foundation for our salvation and also as the touchstone of hope for our eternal life.

3.  The fact that the resurrection of Jesus was observed by multiple eyewitnesses who have left their testimonies behind for others to hear is of great significance. Hundreds of eyewitnesses were involved, and some of

them eventually accepted persecution, torture and death rather than denying their testimony. We can see this in Acts 4:1-17, as well as in other writings outside the New Testament. When we compare the cowardice of the apostles prior to Jesus' death with their boldness after his resurrection it is a stunning turn-around, and in every case but one it led them eventually to give their lives in defense of the truth of Jesus' resurrection.

4. We cannot omit a reference to the case of the apostle Paul. He was among the cruelest of the enemies of Jesus and his followers and among the strongest deniers of their teachings. Yet when he miraculously met the resurrected Jesus on the road to Damascus he experienced an immediate, drastic and permanent change to become one of the strongest defenders of the resurrection in history.

5. The fact that faith in the resurrection of Jesus emerged right there in Jerusalem where he had been entombed was evidence of the truth of the resurrection. If he had remained in the tomb it would have been a simple matter to discover and expose his body for all eyes to see. Some claimed that the disciples stole Jesus' body, but if that were the case we could never explain why they later all offered themselves for torture and death to proclaim his resurrection. Others claimed that Jesus never really died, but only faked his death and later escaped, yet that, too, is absurd.

6. Yet we can still ask the question, does it really matter whether or not Jesus rose from the dead? Some Bible

skeptics today would tell us that what really matters is the faith of the Early Church, and not necessarily that it really happened. But Paul was correct when he told us that if Jesus did not arise from the dead our faith is in vain. The resurrection of Jesus was important because it was the fulfillment of prophecy. Jesus himself had prophesied it (Mark 8:31), as we see also in Psalm 16:10-11 and Isaiah 53:12.

7. Even more significantly, the resurrection of Jesus was necessary because it is the foundation of our salvation. Paul says in Romans 4:23-25, "Now it was not written for his sake alone that it was imputed to him, but also for us. It shall be imputed to us who believe in Him who raised up Jesus our Lord from the dead, who was delivered up because of our offenses, and was raised because of our justification." In the Old Testament the High Priest every year went into the Holy of Holies to offer a sin offering on behalf of the nation, with a rope tied around his leg. If the offering for one reason or the other was unacceptable to Yahweh, the High Priest would not come out alive but would have to be pulled out by the rope. But if he reappeared alive at the door of the Holy of Holies a shout of praise would ascend among the people. In like manner, Jesus appears alive at the door of an empty tomb, signaling that God the Father had accepted his offering once and for all and for all humanity (Heb. 9:11-15).

8. Finally, let us note that the resurrection of Jesus is the guarantee that we, too, will one day be resurrected. For all of us there is something naturally foreboding about

death. Death takes us into an unknown world, from which no one whom we know has ever returned. We are like babies in a mother's womb, where we are warm, protected and comfortable. Yet it is only through the trauma of birth that babies can emerge into what is a much better world, with untold greater possibilities for movement, freedom, sight and adventure. Paul says, "But now Christ is risen from the dead, *and* has become the firstfruits of those who have fallen asleep" (1 Cor. 15:20). We, too, will one day be resurrected into a world far greater than we have ever known on this planet Earth. Praise to our great God for the resurrected Jesus!

## Questions

1. Why did Jesus rebuke Peter at Caesarea Philippi, and what did it have to do with the resurrection?

2. What is the significance of the fact that hundreds of people saw Jesus after he was resurrected?

3. What was it that so powerfully convinced Paul to follow Jesus?

4. What does Paul mean when he says our faith is vain if Christ was not resurrected?

5. How does the resurrection of Jesus relate to our own future resurrection?

## Things to Think About

❖ *Christianity is the only world religion with a resurrected Savior.*

❖ *It is impossible to accept the truth of the resurrection of Jesus without also acknowledging that he is the Son of God.*

# THE SECOND COMING OF JESUS

Acts 1:10-11; Hebrews 9:28; Revelation 19:11-16

*And while they looked steadfastly toward heaven as He went up, behold, two men stood by them in white apparel, who also said, "Men of Galilee, why do you stand gazing up into heaven? This same Jesus, who was taken up from you into heaven, will so come in like manner as you saw Him go into heaven." . . . so Christ was offered once to bear the sins of many. To those who eagerly wait for Him He will appear a second time, apart from sin, for salvation. . . . Now I saw heaven opened, and behold, a white horse. And He who sat on him was called Faithful and True, and in righteousness He judges and makes war. His eyes were like a flame of fire, and on His head were many crowns. He had a name written that no one knew except Himself. He was clothed with a robe dipped in blood, and His name is called The Word of God. And the armies in heaven, clothed in fine linen, white and clean, followed Him on white horses. Now out of His mouth goes a sharp sword, that with it He should strike the nations. And He Himself will rule them with a rod of iron. He Himself treads the winepress of the fierceness and wrath of Almighty God. And He has on His robe and on His thigh a name written: KING OF KINGS AND LORD OF LORDS.*

## Lesson Theme

Strong belief in the Second Coming of Jesus has always been a mark of vibrant Christianity. When Christian faith and fervor diminish, so also does conviction about the promise of Christ's return. Jesus' Parable of the Ten Virgins illustrates the reality of wise virgins faithfully awaiting the return of the Master, with their lamps trimmed and burning. It also depicts five foolish virgins slumbering and sleeping with their lamps burning low. In this and other parables Jesus taught his followers to expect him to one day return to earth. That is why, as Jesus ascended into heaven on a hill near Jerusalem, forty days after his resurrection, angels announced to his followers, ""Men of Galilee, why do you stand gazing up into heaven? This *same* Jesus, who was taken up from you into heaven, will so come in like manner as you saw Him go into heaven" (Acts 1:11).

## Introduction

As we will see in this lesson, there are an abundance of promises in the scriptures that Jesus will one day return to earth in a great Second Coming. The pertinent question, then, is this: Does God keep his promises? How can we be sure that all of the promises of a Second Coming should be taken seriously? One of the answers surely is to study the fact that for many long centuries there were Old Testament prophecies about the First Coming of Jesus. The birth of a

Messiah was predicted even with many of its details: where he would be born, that he would be born of a virgin mother, that he would suffer rejection and cruelty, that he would be crucified, etc. All of those promises were eventually fulfilled in complete detail and complete accuracy. Likewise, we can be sure of the fulfillment of the promises of the Second Coming. In this lesson we will see some of the details about what that means.

## Lesson

1. At his first coming, Jesus came to this earth as a baby in a manger and eventually as the suffering Servant about whom Isaiah wrote over 700 years earlier. However, at his Second Coming it will be amazingly different. Jesus will come as a conquering king. He will come with the great armies of the heavenly hosts. John shows the grandeur and majesty of that Second Coming in clear details in Revelation 19:11-16. "Now I saw heaven opened, and behold, a white horse. And He who sat on him *was* called Faithful and True, and in righteousness He judges and makes war. His eyes *were* like a flame of fire, and on His head *were* many crowns. He had a name written that no one knew except Himself. He *was* clothed with a robe dipped in blood, and His name is called The Word of God. And the armies in heaven, clothed in fine linen, white and clean, followed Him on white horses. Now out of His mouth goes a sharp sword, that with it He should strike the nations. And He Himself will rule them with a rod of iron. He Himself treads the winepress of the fierceness and wrath of Almighty God. And He has on *His* robe and on

His thigh a name written: KING OF KINGS AND LORD OF LORDS."

**"To those who eagerly wait for Him He will appear a second time, apart from sin, for salvation" (Heb. 9:28).**

2. Prophecies of the Second Coming (sometimes called the Second Advent) of Jesus can be found in both the Old Testament and the New Testament. However, in the Old Testament at times it is difficult to see a clear distinction between the two events. For example, Isaiah 7:14 is clearly a description of Jesus coming as a baby born to a virgin ("Behold, the virgin shall conceive. . . ."). Yet the coming of Jesus is also described in Isaiah 9:6-7 not as a baby or as a suffering servant, but as that of a conquering king ("The government shall be upon His shoulder," and "of the increase of His government and peace there shall be no end"). These words are obviously describing the Second Coming of Jesus, when he will return to earth as a conquering king.

3. Zechariah gave several prophecies about the Second Coming of the Messiah, such as Zechariah 9:14 ("The Lord God will blow the trumpet, and go with whirlwinds from the south). Amos 9:14 prophecies what will happen at the Second Coming: "I will bring back the captives of My people Israel; they shall build the waste cities and inhabit *them." Joel 3:1-2 speaks in similar terms, obviously referring not to the first coming of Jesus, but to the Second Coming:* "For behold, in those days and at that time, when I bring back the captives of Judah and Jerusalem, I will also gather all nations, and bring them down to the Valley of Jehoshaphat."

4. There are several purposes that will bc achieved with the Second Coming of Jesus. Matthew 16:27 says that Jesus will come "in the glory of His Father." As he thus comes, he will clearly divide the sheep from the goats. "Then two *men* will be in the field: one will be taken and the other left" (Mat. 24:40). His coming will mark the end of human probation, as he comes to judge the wicked and to redeem his saints (Mat. 16:27; 1 John 3:2).

5. The Bible speaks of a number of events that surround the Second Coming of Jesus. There are a multitude of differing opinions about the relationship between those events and those who are involved: the tribulation, the Antichrist, the "man of lawlessness," the false prophet, the "restrainer," the rapture, and the millennium. Many Bible scholars make a distinction between the rapture and the Second Coming, but some do not. Some teach that a great tribulation will proceed

the Second Coming, but others do not. Some believe that a thousand-year reign of righteousness (Rev. 20:6) will come only after the return of Jesus, and others do not. These are not matters over which believers should quarrel or divide.

6. One of the most persistent questions about the Second Coming of Jesus is about its timing. When will Jesus return? Is it possible to know when Jesus is coming back? This is the type of questions Jesus' disciples asked him in Matthew 24:3. "Tell us, when will these things be? And what *will be* the sign of Your coming, and of the end of the age?" It is important to note that in the sermon that follows in Matthew 24 and 25 Jesus repeatedly tells his disciples that "no one knows" the exact timing of the Second Coming. It is clear that for reasons we may not understand God does not want us to know the answer to that question. This is why we should take seriously the words of Jesus, "Therefore you also be ready, for the Son of Man is coming at an hour you do not expect" (Mat. 24:44).

7. The note of caution that we should all heed here is that despite the clear statements of Jesus that no one knows the date of the Second Coming there has been a very long list of individuals throughout Christian history who have attempted to gather followers by making bold prophecies with specific dates for Christ's return. Needless to say, every such prophecy has been proven wrong. Those who attempt to continue to make such prophecies should be steadfastly avoided. Our own

stand must simply be to be watchful and to be ready for the Lord's return at any moment.

8. We are still left with the question about whether the Second Coming of Jesus can be said to be *imminent*. Is it accurate to say that Jesus will come back *soon*? In every age of the Church there have been at least some who have believed that the Second Coming of Jesus would surely happen very soon. Again and again they have been proven wrong. However, James did tell his readers, "You also be patient. Establish your hearts, for the coming of the Lord is at hand" (James 5:8). Our best advice is to heed Jesus' admonition: "Therefore you also be ready, for the Son of Man is coming at an hour you do not expect" (Luke 12:40). Jesus is coming again! We can be sure that we serve a great God who will not fail to send his beloved Son, Jesus Christ, back to earth at exactly the right moment.

## Questions

1. How would you describe the difference between the Jesus we see in his first coming and the Jesus we will see in his Second Coming?

2. What are some of the promises of Jesus' Second Coming found in the Old Testament?

3. What are some of the events and actors surrounding the Second Coming?

4. Why do you think people in every Christian age have tried to set specific dates for the return of Jesus?

5. Do you think it is accurate to say that Jesus will come back soon?

## Things to Think About

❖ *Even in Paul's day people were already wasting time worrying and speculating about events surrounding the promised return of Christ, as we see in his letters to the Thessalonians.*

❖ *Let us be prepared for Jesus to come back at any moment; but let us also work and plan as though his coming could be delayed for another 100 years.*

# PART
# FOUR

# THE HOLY SPIRIT

It has been argued by some Christians that the Holy Spirit is the least studied, the least understood and the least worshipped of the three Persons in the Holy Trinity. God the Father is clearly seen and highlighted in both the Old Testament and in the New Testament. God the Son may not be fully revealed in the Old Testament, but he is anticipated there; and in the New Testament he is center stage, because of the incarnation. Yet we see little about the Holy Spirit in the Old Testament, and only toward the end of the gospels and in the Book of Acts do we see more about the Third Person of the Trinity.

There are many misunderstandings about the Holy Spirit. Some have taught that he is not a Person as the other members of the Trinity, but only some kind of force or power. Yet the Bible makes it clear that the Holy Spirit is truly God and is rightfully understood as part of the Trinity. We can see, for example, that when Peter confronted Ananias in Acts 5 about his sin of both greed and deception, he asked him why he had lied to the Holy Spirit. Peter said to him, "You have not lied to men but to God" (Acts 5:5).

In this final section of our study about our great God we will study about the person and ministry of the Holy Spirit, as revealed in both the Old Testament and the New Testament. Let us pray that we will gain a clear understanding of the importance of worshiping God not only as Father and Son but also as Holy Spirit.

158

# THE HOLY SPIRIT IN THE OLD TESTAMENT

### Genesis 1:1-2; Numbers 27:18; 1 Samuel 16:12-13; Psalm 139:7-8

*In the beginning God created the heavens and the earth. The earth was without form, and void; and darkness was on the face of the deep. And the Spirit of God was hovering over the face of the waters. . . . And the Lord said to Moses: "Take Joshua the son of Nun with you, a man in whom is the Spirit, and lay your hand on him; . . . Now he [David] was ruddy, with bright eyes, and good-looking. And the Lord said, "Arise, anoint him; for this is the one!" Then Samuel took the horn of oil and anointed him in the midst of his brothers; and the Spirit of the Lord came upon David from that day forward. . . . Where can I go from Your Spirit? Or where can I flee from Your presence? If I ascend into heaven, You are there; If I make my bed in [a]hell, behold, You are there.*

## Lesson Theme

It stretches our minds beyond their capacity to realize that the Holy Trinity has existed since before the creation of the world and throughout all of eternity. Yet that is the truth revealed in the Bible. God the Father, God the Son and God the Holy Spirit are eternally one and eternally existent. Therefore, it should not surprise us that in the very opening statements of the Book of Genesis we see not just God the Father, but God the Holy Spirit. "In the beginning God created the heavens and the earth. . . . And the Spirit of God was hovering over the face of the waters" (Gen. 1:1-2). It is true that we do not hear as much about the Holy Spirit in the pages of the Old Testament as we do in the New Testament. However, the Spirit of God was definitely there right from the beginning, and we can see his work here and there throughout the Old Testament. That is what we are examining in this lesson.

## Introduction

There are clear differences between how the Holy Spirit is revealed in the Old Testament and how he is revealed in the New Testament. When we read the words of Jesus to his disciples in John 14 and 16, for example, we can get the feeling that the Holy Spirit was not present in the world before that time. Jesus talked about sending the Holy Spirit, telling his disciples, "Nevertheless I tell you the truth. It is to your advantage that I go away; for if I do not go away, the Helper will not come to you; but if I depart, I will send Him to you" (John 14:7). This "Helper," as all Bible scholars agree, is the Holy Spirit, the Third Person of the Holy Trinity. However, Jesus is not saying that the Holy Spirit had not yet entered the world and was not active in the lives of God's children prior to then, but that in the coming days his role as a Helper or Comforter or Advocate would be more important to the followers of Jesus than ever. What we will see in this lesson is that the Holy Spirit was indeed active in the affairs of earth and of humanity right from the first moments of creation.

## Lesson

1. A close study of the Old Testament shows us that the Holy Spirit was active in a variety of ways prior to the New Testament. We have already seen that it was the Holy Spirit that moved over the waters at the beginning of creation. We can also see that the Holy Spirit was active throughout the Old Testament as the inspirer of prophecy. We read at several points, "The Spirit of God came upon . . ." naming prophets or servants of God such as David, Sampson, Elijah, Gideon, etc. For example, "Then the Spirit of God came upon Zechariah the son of Jehoiada the priest, who stood above the people, and said to them, "Thus says God: . . ." (2 Chron.24:20). David said, "The Spirit of the LORD spoke by me, and His word was on my tongue." The prophet Ezekiel reported, "Then the Spirit entered me when He spoke to me" (Ezek. 2:2). Centuries later, Peter described this role of the Holy Spirit in the Old Testament by saying: "Prophecy never came by the will of man, but holy men of God spoke *as they were* moved by the Holy Spirit" (2 Pet. 1:21).

**The Holy Spirit hovered over the waters at the time of the creation of the world.**

2. What we see is that it was often the Holy Spirit who not only inspired prophecies and the writing of Old Testament scripture, but who was the strengthener of those who represented God. In the Book of Judges, for example, we see again and again that it was the Spirit who strengthened people such as Othniel, Jephthah, Samson and Gideon. It was through the ministry of the Holy Spirit that they were able to lead God's people and protect them against their enemies.

3. The Holy Spirit is also depicted in the Old Testament as equipping certain people with special skills necessary to accomplish work for God and his people. When God directed Moses to undertake the meticulous and difficult task of building the tabernacle in the wilderness he gave him two men who were highly

skilled craftsmen to guide the work, Bezalel and Oholiab. They were the ancient equivalent of today's top engineers or artisans. "See, I have called by name Bezalel the son of Uri, the son of Hur, of the tribe of Judah. And I have filled him with the Spirit of God, in wisdom, in understanding, in knowledge, and in all *manner of* workmanship, to design artistic works, to work in gold, in silver, in bronze, in cutting jewels for setting, in carving wood, and to work in all *manner of* workmanship" (Ex. 31:2-4). The key point here is that it was the special work of the Holy Spirit to equip these men for their important work.

4.  We discover in the New Testament that one of the ministries of the Holy Spirit is to convince people about sin. Jesus said concerning the ministry of the Holy Spirit especially after his own departure that "when He has come, He will convict the world of sin, and of righteousness, and of judgment" (John 16:8). However, there is clear evidence that this ministry of the Holy Spirit in convicting of sin was present even during Old Testament times. For example, Genesis 6:3 says regarding the rise of sin prior to the Great Flood, "And the Lord said, 'My Spirit shall not strive with man forever, for he *is* indeed flesh; yet his days shall be one hundred and twenty years.'" Among unbelievers it is clear that the Holy Spirit was acting as a restraining influence. The Holy Spirit was at work striving to draw people to righteousness and away from ungodliness, even though God's wrath finally was exhausted at the time of the Great Flood.

5. Unlike in the New Testament, there is no promise of the permanent indwelling of believers by the Holy Spirit in Old Testament times. What we see is that the Holy Spirit came upon people for the accomplishment of certain responsibilities. It was said of Othniel, for example, "The Spirit of the LORD came upon him, and he judged Israel" (Judg. 3:10). In 1 Samuel 10:10 we see Saul prophesying among the prophets because "the Spirit of God came upon him." Later, 1 Samuel 16:14 says, "But the Spirit of the Lord departed from Saul, and a distressing spirit from the Lord troubled him."

6. We can conclude that though the Bible does not give us a complete view of the work of the Holy Spirit during the Old Testament period he was definitely present and active throughout that time. Though the Holy Spirit gave special anointing for special tasks it is evident that such anointing could be given and then later withdrawn. Certainly, we see that during the Old Testament period the Holy Spirit gave some believers special abilities for the performance of work given to them by God.

7. In our next lesson we will see more about the differences between the work of the Holy Spirit in the Old Testament and in the New Testament. We cannot say that great Bible heroes such as Moses or Daniel or Elijah were less godly and holy people than those who lived in New Testament times or in later generations. They were men who lived in the power of the Holy

Spirit. But we will see that there were also benefits that were made more visible for all of God's people through the revelation God and through the work of the Holy Spirit as revealed in the New Testament.

## Questions

1. Name some of the ways in which the Holy Spirit was active in Old Testament times.

2. Describe the ministry of the Holy Spirit in the writing of Old Testament scripture.

3. Why was the work of the Holy Spirit important in the life of Bezalel (Exodus 31)?

4. What is the meaning behind the words, "My Spirit will not strive with man forever" (Genesis 6:3)?

5. What difference do you see between the ministry of the Holy Spirit in the Old Testament and in the New Testament?

## Things to Think About

❖ *Without the breath of the Holy Spirit on the Holy Scriptures (2 Tim. 3:16; 2 Pet. 1:21) we would have no sure foundation for our understanding of eternal truth.*

❖ *We must never fail to appreciate the faithful ministry of the Holy Spirit in restraining sin and revealing truth.*

OUR GREAT GOD

# THE PROMISES OF THE SPIRIT'S COMING

Isaiah 32:15; Ezekiel 36:26-27; Joel 2:28-29; John 14:15-17

*Until the Spirit is poured upon us from on high, and the wilderness becomes a fruitful field, and the fruitful field is counted as a forest. . . . I will give you a new heart and put a new spirit within you; I will take the heart of stone out of your flesh and give you a heart of flesh. I will put My Spirit within you and cause you to walk in My statutes, and you will keep My judgments and do them. . . . "And it shall come to pass afterward that I will pour out My Spirit on all flesh; your sons and your daughters shall prophesy, your old men shall dream dreams, your young men shall see visions. And also on My menservants and on My maidservants I will pour out My Spirit in those days. . . . "If you love Me, keep My commandments. And I will pray the Father, and He will give you another Helper, that He may abide with you forever the Spirit of truth, whom the world cannot receive, because it neither sees Him nor knows Him; but you know Him, for He dwells with you and will be in you.*

## Lesson Theme

One of the most important prophecies in scripture is what John the Baptist proclaimed at the baptism of Jesus, in the Jordan River. At that point Jesus had not yet entered into his three-year ministry. This was the first recorded announcement we know about of what was soon to come. John's words were a clear echo of the prophecy of Malachi 400 years earlier. Malachi spoke of John the Baptist's ministry in these terms: ""Behold, I send My messenger, and he will prepare the way before Me. And the Lord [i.e., Jesus], whom you seek, will suddenly come to His temple" (Mal 3:1). Of the ministry of Jesus, Malachi had further proclaimed, "He *is* like a refiner's fire and like launderers' soap. He will sit as a refiner and a purifier of silver" (vv. 2-3). John, preaching in the wilderness, cried out in prophetic mode, "I indeed baptize you with water unto repentance, but He who is coming after me is mightier than I, whose sandals I am not worthy to carry. He will baptize you with the Holy Spirit and fire" (Mat. 3:11). John saw that one of the greatest works of Jesus Christ, the Son of God, was to usher in a new phase of the work of the Holy Spirit. It is no wonder that at the baptism of Jesus we see a clear picture of the Trinity. Jesus, the Son of God, is baptized. The Holy Spirit descends in the form of a dove. The Father speaks approval from above: ""This is My beloved Son, in whom I am well pleased" (Mat. 3:17).

## Introduction

Prophecies of the appearance and workings of the Holy Spirit are present in many places throughout the scriptures.

In this lesson we will look at some of the most noteworthy, starting with the Old Testament prophets and moving finally to the words of Jesus. What we are particularly focusing on is what we may describe as the more evident and open and universal outpouring of the Holy Spirit that was introduced on the Day of Pentecost. It is clear when we read John's words at the baptism of Jesus that he was referring to the special baptism of fire that would be received on the 120 disciples as they tarried in the Upper Room in Jerusalem. Yet we can also read similar allusions right from the time of the earlier Old Testament prophets. Let us look at some of those expectations in this lesson.

## Lesson

1. We will look at three of the so-called Major Prophets in the Old Testament (sometimes referred to as the Latter Prophets) who spoke boldly about the coming of the Holy Spirit in a future age. The Major Prophets include Isaiah, Jeremiah, Ezekiel and Daniel. We call them major not because they were necessarily more important than the "minor prophets" (Joel, Amos, Obadiah, etc.) but because their written prophecies within our Bibles are much longer. For example, the Book of Jeremiah, by word-count, is the longest book in the Bible. First, though, consider what the Prophet Isaiah says about the coming of the Holy Spirit. In Isaiah 32:15 he says, "Until the Spirit is poured upon us from on high, and the wilderness becomes a fruitful field, and the fruitful field is counted as a forest." Later, in Isaiah 44:2-3 he says, "Thus says the Lord who made you and formed you from the womb, . . . 'I will pour

water on him who is thirsty, and floods on the dry ground; I will pour My Spirit on your descendants, and My blessing on your offspring." Isaiah was clearly looking ahead to a day when the Holy Spirit would be poured out as never before, and which was fulfilled eventually on the Day of Pentecost.

**Malachi described the coming Messiah as launderer's soap and a refiner of silver.**

2. In the case of Jeremiah, we do not see direct references to the coming of the Holy Spirit in the lives of believers. However, we do see clear statement from Jeremiah about the nature of a new form of God's covenant to his people. In Jeremiah 31:31 he prophecies, "Behold, the days are coming, says the Lord, when I will make a new covenant with the house of Israel and with the house of Judah." That new covenant was not a fundamental re-writing of the law of God, but that it would now be written on the hearts of believers. "But this *is* the covenant that I will make with the house of Israel after those days, says the Lord: I will put My law in their

minds, and write it on their hearts; and I will be their God, and they shall be My people. No more shall every man teach his neighbor, and every man his brother, saying, 'Know the Lord,' for they all shall know Me, from the least of them to the greatest of them, says the Lord" (Jer. 31:33-34).

3. It is when we turn to Ezekiel's prophecies that we see far clearer prophecies of the outpouring of the Holy Spirit that was to come along with the new covenant prophesied by Jeremiah. Ezekiel lived 150 years after the time of Isaiah and around 50 years after Jeremiah. He experienced the devastation of the Great Exile and the return of some of the Jewish people to their homeland. It was in that context that he peered prophetically into the future and saw the importance of the future outpouring of the Holy Spirit. Through Ezekiel God said, "I will sprinkle clean water on you, and you shall be clean; I will cleanse you from all your filthiness and from all your idols. I will give you a new heart and put a new spirit within you; I will take the heart of stone out of your flesh and give you a heart of flesh. I will put My Spirit within you and cause you to walk in My statutes, and you will keep My judgments and do *them" (Ezek. 36:25-27)*.

4. In the following chapter, speaking of his vision of the Valley of Dry Bones, God says through the prophet, "I will put My Spirit in you, and you shall live, and I will place you in your own land" (Ezek. 37:14). And yet later Ezekiel writes, similarly, "I will not hide My face from them anymore; for I shall have poured out My Spirit on

the house of Israel,' says the Lord God" (Ezek. 39:29). The prophecy of the coming of the Holy Spirit in a way never experienced within the Old Testament era was clearly revealed.

5. There are similar prophecies within the so-called Minor Prophets. One of the most notable is the prophecy of Joel, which came even before that of Isaiah, more than 800 years before New Testament times. So clear was Joel's prophecy that on the Day of Pentecost people, as the Holy Spirit was poured out on the 120 in the Upper Room, Peter cried out, "This is what was spoken by the prophet Joel" (Acts 2:16). "And it shall come to pass afterward that I will pour out My Spirit on all flesh; your sons and your daughters shall prophesy, your old men shall dream dreams, your young men shall see visions. And also on *My* menservants and on *My* maidservants I will pour out My Spirit in those days" (Joel 2:28-29).

6. We have already seen from Malachi's prophecy his references to the coming work of the Holy Spirit in the fiery baptism of God's people, as one sent by both the Father and the Son. Jesus told his disciples, "But when the Helper comes, whom I shall send to you from the Father, the Spirit of truth who proceeds from the Father, He will testify of Me" (John 15:26). Malachi's expression of Jesus, therefore, was that "He will sit as a refiner and a purifier of silver; He will purify the sons of Levi, and purge them as gold and silver, that they may offer to the Lord an offering in righteousness" (Mal. 3:3).

7.  Jesus' ministry to his disciples was filled with wonderful teaching, powerful miracles, great demonstrations of teaching, preaching and healing, and finally great promises for the future. As Jesus spent his last hours with his disciples prior to his trial, crucifixion and resurrection, he took time to explain to them the importance of the coming of the Holy Spirit at Pentecost. He told them,  "I will pray the Father, and He will give you another Helper, that He may abide with you forever the Spirit of truth, whom the world cannot receive, because it neither sees Him nor knows Him; but you know Him, for He dwells with you and will be in you" (John 14:16-17). Though they surely could not have understood all he meant by it, Jesus added, "It is to your advantage that I go away; for if I do not go away, the Helper will not come to you; but if I depart, I will send Him to you" (John 16:7). It is clear that Jesus was speaking in full harmony with what the prophets before him had said: God would one day send the Holy Spirit in such a way that he would be poured out upon all the people of God. That would be the very fire that would ignite the Church and send it out to conquer the world.

8.  The final commission of Jesus regarding the coming of the Holy Spirit is found in the first chapter of Acts. Jesus had told them in what we often refer to as the Great Commission that they should go and make disciples of all nations, baptizing them in the name of the Father, the Son and the Holy Spirit (Mat. 28:18-20). But now, as Jesus is nearing the time of his departure he

issues one final command. He told them, "John truly baptized with water, but you shall be baptized with the Holy Spirit not many days from now" (Acts 1:5). Then he said, "You shall receive power when the Holy Spirit has come upon you; and you shall be witnesses to Me in Jerusalem, and in all Judea and Samaria, and to the end of the earth" (Acts 1:8).

9.  With those words Jesus was saying the final "amen" to what had been said hundreds of years earlier by Isaiah, Jeremiah, Ezekiel, Joel, Malachi, and three years earlier by John the Baptist. It only remained for the disciples to heed Jesus' command and tarry in the Upper Room before fires would be ignited that took them (and us, too) to Jerusalem, Judea, Samaria and the end of the earth. Praise God!

## Questions

1.  Why do you believe John the Baptist talked about baptism by fire when he summarized the ministry of Jesus?

2.  What did Jeremiah say about the new thing that was to come in the future for God's people?

3.  What was the power behind the reviving of the dry bones in Ezekiel's vision in chapter 37?

4.  What Old Testament prophet did Peter quote on the Day of Pentecost, and for what reason?

5. Why do you believe Jesus was so eager to explain the coming of the Holy Spirit to his disciples?"

## Things to Think About

❖ *Just as the spotlight was on the work of Jesus Christ during his earthly ministry, so the spotlight during the emergence of the Early Church was on the work of the Holy Spirit.*

❖ *Every believer today has the same privilege as the early disciples to experience the outpouring of the Holy Spirit and the privilege to walk in his empowerment.*

# OUR GREAT GOD

# THE IMPORTANCE OF PENTECOST

### Luke 24:49; Acts 1:8; 2:1-4; 15:8-9

*Behold, I send the Promise of My Father upon you; but tarry in the city of Jerusalem until you are endued with power from on high." . . . But you shall receive power when the Holy Spirit has come upon you; and you shall be witnesses to Me in Jerusalem, and in all Judea and Samaria, and to the end of the earth." . . . When the Day of Pentecost had fully come, they were all with one accord in one place. And suddenly there came a sound from heaven, as of a rushing mighty wind, and it filled the whole house where they were sitting. Then there appeared to them divided tongues, as of fire, and one sat upon each of them. And they were all filled with the Holy Spirit and began to speak with other tongues, as the Spirit gave them utterance. . . . So God, who knows the heart, acknowledged them by giving them the Holy Spirit, just as He did to us, and made no distinction between us and them, purifying their hearts by faith.*

## Lesson Theme

As we have seen in our previous lessons, there were multiple promises of a special outpouring of the Holy Spirit, starting from the time of the Old Testament prophets. Those promises were repeated by John the Baptist and Jesus. We have seen that the final instructions of Jesus to his disciples included both the Great Commission (to go to the ends of the earth making disciples) and specific instructions to first "tarry in the city of Jerusalem until you are endued with power from on high" (Luke 24:49). Luke tells us that the disciples obeyed the command to remain in Jerusalem, and after 120 of them waited for ten days in a large room the Holy Spirit descended on them in one of the most remarkable events in the pages of the Bible. Acts 2:1-31 gives us a riveting account of what happened on that historic day. They were celebrating the Feast of Weeks, as prescribed in Jewish law, but we now know that what was happening was in reality the birth of the Christian Church. In this lesson we will understand what actually happened at Pentecost and why it is so important for believers even today.

## Introduction

The word *Pentecost* comes from a Greek word meaning "fiftieth," because it marked a festival celebrated on the fiftieth day after the Jewish Passover. The Jewish Festival of Weeks (marking the time of harvest, or first-fruits) was celebrated at that point on the calendar. What we read in Acts 2 is that on that day, after waiting in the large room for ten days, they were all in "one accord" and suddenly there was the sound from heaven as of a "rushing mighty wind" that filled the entire room. "Divided tongues of fire" sat on each of them. Luke says that at that point they were all filled with the Holy Spirit and then began to speak in languages they had not known before, "as the Spirit gave them utterance" (Acts 2:1-4). The result was that on that day alone, after the fiery preaching of Peter, 3,000 people gave their lives to Jesus and were baptized. What an incredible and wonderful day marked the birthday of the Christian Church! We call it Pentecost.

## Lesson

1. The prophet Joel had made a remarkable prophecy about Pentecost hundreds of years earlier: "It shall come to pass afterward that I will pour out My Spirit on all flesh" (Joel 2:28). That prophecy received remarkable fulfillment in the Upper Room on the Day of Pentecost. As Peter preached he made specific reference to Joel's long-ago prophecy. From that point forward, the Holy Spirit would come in to dwell in the hearts of those who received Jesus Christ as their Savior. Here was a major difference from the role of the Holy Spirit in the Old Testament, where we have seen that he empowered people for specific tasks and for specific periods of time. Now, on the Day of Pentecost, the early Christians began to experience the continual abiding presence of the Holy Spirit, just as Jesus had promised in John 14:16, when he said, "I will pray the Father, and He will give you another Helper, that He may abide with you forever." Peter promised that same abiding presence of the Holy Spirit to thousands of

people who heard his Pentecost sermon. He said, "Repent, and let every one of you be baptized in the name of Jesus Christ for the remission of sins; and you shall receive the gift of the Holy Spirit" (Acts 2:38).

**The Day of Pentecost witnessed the long-promised outpouring of the Holy Spirit, accompanied by symbolic signs and wonders.**

2. There was a lot of important symbolism attached to this historic Pentecostal outpouring of the Holy Spirit. It is important that we understand what was symbolic and what was essential. First, there was the symbol of a sound as of a great wind. Both in the Old Testament and the New Testament wind is a symbol of the Holy Spirit. The Old Testament Hebrew word *ruach*, and the New Testament Greek word *pneuma* both refer to the Holy Spirit. They are both translated "wind." The sound of a rushing wind was symbolic of the arrival of the Holy Spirit. The cloven or divided tongues of fire were what Luke says were *like* fire (NET) or *seemed to be* (NIV) or

*appeared to them* (NASB) as fire, which tells us that it was not actual fire but symbolic of fire. This is no doubt the fiery cleansing that had been prophesied by Malachi, John and Jesus.

3. The symbolism of miraculous communication in multiple languages was a third powerful symbol. Present at Pentecost were Jews from eighteen different linguistic regions in the Jewish diaspora. As the 120 were caught up with the outpouring of the Holy Spirit suddenly the Holy Spirit "gave them utterance" (Acts 2:4) to begin to praise the mighty works of God. They were speaking not in their native tongues or even in the Greek language shared by many throughout the Roman Empire of the time or the Aramaic language spoken by Jews living in Jerusalem, but in the tongues represented among the visiting diaspora Jews. It was a sheer miracle of communication that symbolized the universal destiny of the ministry of the Holy Spirit throughout the Church. Onlookers were amazed by this unprecedented miracle, saying, "How *is it that* we hear, each in our own language in which we were born?" (Acts 2:8). Others assumed the 120 were just drunk (v. 12).

4. Beneath all of this important symbolism were two essential facts. The Holy Spirit was now being poured out universally on God's people, and his fiery presence was accomplishing a deep cleansing of their hearts. This is exactly what Peter testified to some twelve years later, at the famous Jerusalem Council reported in Acts 15. There Peter was called on the carpet over the fact

that Gentiles were being ushered into this new faith under his ministry. As he defended his own actions at Caesarea, in the house of the Roman centurion Cornelius, Peter indirectly testified not only to what happened to Cornelius, but what had happened years before in Jerusalem in that Upper Room. Peter said to the council: "So God, who knows the heart, acknowledged them by giving them the Holy Spirit, just as *He did* to us, and made no distinction between us and them, <u>purifying their hearts by faith</u>" (Acts 15:8-9). The essence of Pentecost is the outpouring of the Holy Spirit as he cleanses the hearts of believers, by faith.

5. How is the Pentecost we read about in the Bible related to the Pentecostal movement of modern times? We should not forget that Christians of all persuasions celebrate to one degree or the other the importance of what happened at Pentecost, as recorded in the Acts of the Apostles. However, Pentecostal Christians of modern times place a strong focus on the importance of experiencing a personal powerful outpouring of the Holy Spirit, usually accompanied by speaking in tongues (though usually not a known human language like we see in Acts 2). Modern Pentecostalism started over 100 years ago as a small movement, yet it eventually became the fastest growing movement in global Christianity, and today counts more than one-half billion adherents all over the world. It is the greatest religious movement and phenomenon of modern times.

6. What are the lessons we should all learn about the spiritual significance of Pentecost? What we are seeing here is not just about something that happened to 120 people some 2,000 years ago. There are important lessons for us to apply to our own lives. First is that the power and presence of the Holy Spirit is absolutely essential for Christian success. We must all live and move in the power of the Holy Spirit. We must be freed from the slavery of sin and experience the cleansing Peter talked about in Acts 15:8-9. Nothing else can substitute for the power and presence of the Holy Spirit in our lives.

7. Pentecost was the birth of the Christian Church. Pentecost therefore teaches us that God's plan and purpose is that the Church should be at the center of his expanding global kingdom. The Church started small, but even at the outset, Luke noted that "The Lord added to the church daily those who were being saved" (Acts 2:47). That is what has been happening ever since. It means that as believers we must not only be filled with the Holy Spirit, but we must also be a conscious part of the active, growing, multiplying and triumphant Church.

8. Pentecost also teaches us that the mission of the Church is and must always be a universal one. The focus on the speaking of many languages on the Day of Pentecost is a powerful reminder that the Church must surely reach every tribe or ethnicity in every country of the world. That is what motivated Jesus to say in his Olivet Discourse, "This gospel of the kingdom will be

preached in all the world as a witness to all the nations, and then the end will come" (Mat. 24:14). All too often the Church has become divided over language and ethnicity. The power of the Holy Spirit released at Pentecost reminds us to make sure we are continually moving beyond our own language and culture.

9. Finally, Pentecost reminds us that the outpouring of the Holy Spirit is for all classes of people, at all times and in all places. We have seen that in the Old Testament the Holy Spirit came upon special people for special needs and special seasons of time. With Pentecost, however, the doors have been thrown wide open to encompass all of us, at all times, wherever we are. The question for each of us is, Am I right now serving God through the power of the Holy Spirit? Am I a part of the Pentecost movement (no matter what church I may be attending) that was released 2,000 years ago?

## Questions

1. What is the meaning of the word *Pentecost*, and how does it relate to Jewish celebrations?

2. What were the three symbolic signs and wonders at Pentecost and what did each of them represent?

3. What were the two essential facts underlying the signs and wonders of Pentecost?

4. Why do you believe we normally regard Pentecost as the birth of the Christian Church?

5. What are some of the lessons we can learn from Pentecost as applied to our own spiritual lives?

## Things to Think About

❖ *Without Pentecost, Christianity might have become a mere footnote in human history.*

❖ *The recapturing of the spirit and reality of Pentecost is important for Christians of all persuasion, and not just for modern Pentecostals.*

186

# THE BAPTISM AND FULLNESS OF THE HOLY SPIRIT

### Matthew 3:11; Acts 13:9; 1 Corinthians 12:13; Ephesians 5:18

*I indeed baptize you with water unto repentance, but He who is coming after me is mightier than I, whose sandals I am not worthy to carry. He will baptize you with the Holy Spirit and fire. . . . But Saul, who was also known as Paul, filled with the Holy Spirit, fixed his gaze on him, . . . For by one Spirit we were all baptized into one body — whether Jews or Greeks, whether slaves or free — and have all been made to drink into one Spirit. . . . And do not be drunk with wine, in which is dissipation; but be filled with the Spirit.*

## Lesson Theme

Keen attention to the biblical teachings about the baptism with the Holy Spirit and the fulness of the Holy Spirit has been raised in modern times especially by Pentecostalism and the Holiness Movement out of which it emerged over 100 years ago. The followers of John Wesley, especially in America, taught that all believers should experience a deeper heart cleansing and fullness of the Holy Spirit at some point after their conversion. John Wesley referred to that deeper cleansing as "Christian perfection," or "entire sanctification." He did not teach "sinless perfection," as many of his detractors have claimed. Yet he was convinced both by scripture and practical observation that believers could experience a deeper cleansing and freedom from inherited depravity. He was convinced there should be a point of momentary deeper cleansing in the believer's life. Eventually, many years after his death, the Holiness Movement that emerged among his followers began to refer to that moment of deeper cleansing as the Baptism with the Holy Spirit. Therefore, while Wesley believed that Holy Spirit baptism was received at the time of one's conversion, many of his later followers differed. We cannot hope to solve all of these theological issues. In this lesson we will see how both the baptism with the Holy Spirit and the fulness of the Holy Spirit are described within the scriptures.

## Introduction

Building on the teaching of the Holiness Movement that the Baptism with the Holy Spirit is a distinct spiritual experience after conversion, the Pentecostal Movement added the teaching that the Baptism of the Holy Spirit is evidenced by speaking in tongues. Pentecostals believed that the experience described in Acts 2 was an outpouring of the Holy Spirit available not just to 120 people in the Upper Room in Jerusalem but to all believers, everywhere and at all times. That experience is further validated by glossolalia, or speaking in tongues. Pentecostals today are not in agreement on all the details, yet Pentecostalism has become the largest religious movement in Christian history, with over 600 million followers around the world. At the same time, because of this great movement all of modern Christianity has begun to take more seriously the Bible teachings about the baptism with the Holy Spirit and what the fullness of the Holy Spirit means for us today. That is what we want to look at in this lesson.

## Lesson

1.  We saw in Lesson Nineteen that one of the evidences of the presence of the Holy Spirit during Old Testament times was that certain people experienced an infilling or indwelling presence of the Holy Spirit. God said to Moses, in Exodus 28:3, "So you shall speak to all *who are* gifted artisans, whom I have filled with the spirit of wisdom." With reference to Bezalel, who became the primary artisan in charge of the building of the tabernacle, God said, "I have called by name Bezalel . . . I have filled him with the Spirit of God, in wisdom, in understanding, in knowledge, and in all *manner of workmanship*" (Ex. 31:2-3). This same type of infilling of the Holy Spirit was true of John the Baptist. The angel told his father, Zacharias, "He will also be filled with the Holy Spirit, even from his mother's womb" (Luke 1:15). This fullness of the Holy Spirit, or indwelling, is what we might call *charismatic fullness*. It is Holy Spirit presence, filling or anointing as a gift for the accomplishment of a God-given task. It is quite distinct from the baptism with the Holy Spirit, which we will see later.

**The need of every child of Adam and Eve is to experience the baptism with the Holy Spirit and to go on to a life of purity and power.**

2. People with the fulness of the Holy Spirit are working, walking and ministering in the power of the Holy Spirit. They experience unique divine enablement, often for the accomplishment of a specific task. Such fulness was experienced in Old Testament times, but also in later times. The empowering presence of the Holy Spirit for specific ministry purposes that was experienced by people such as Bezalel in Old Testament times is what was identified in the New Testament as the "gifts of the Holy Spirit." Some of such gifts are enumerated in 1 Corinthians 12:8-10, Romans 12:6-8 and 1 Peter 4:11.

3. Aside from this *charismatic* fullness of the Holy Spirit we can also see a scriptural focus on the *ethical* fulness of the Holy Spirit. The focus here is not so much on empowerment or enablement for specific tasks or ministry but more on ethical cleansing, or purity. We have already noted that at Pentecost the 120 were filled

with the Holy Spirit and Peter later testified that the essence of what happened was that their hearts were "purified by faith" (Acts 15:9). The symbolism of fire at Pentecost, which marked the infilling of the Spirit, was the "refiner's fire" sent by God to "purify the sons of Levi" (Mal. 3:3). It was also the fulfillment of John the Baptist's prophecy that Jesus would one day (though the Holy Spirit) baptize his people "with the Holy Spirit and fire" (Mat. 3:11).

4. We must still ask another question. When does the baptism of the Holy Spirit occur? Here we must be careful, because there is plenty of room for misunderstanding and disagreement among contemporary interpreters of the scripture and human experience. We can approach the answer, however, by first asking what is the role of the Holy Spirit in human salvation? At what point does the Holy Spirit enter the life of a believer? The answer from scripture is clear: To be born again is the be *born of the Spirit.* In referring to the new birth and contrasting it with our natural birth, Jesus said to Nicodemus, "That which is born of the flesh is flesh, and that which is born of the Spirit is spirit" (John 3:6). To suggest that born again believers do not have the Holy Spirit living in and working through them and that they only receive the Holy Spirit at a later point is contrary to the teaching of the Bible. The moment we are born again the Holy Spirit lives within us and our bodies are now the "temple of the Holy Spirit" (1 Cor. 6:19-20).

5. Sincere and godly Christian teachers who hold the scriptures in high esteem do not always agree on when the baptism of the Holy Spirit occurs in our Christian journey. Since we all receive the Holy Spirit at our new birth there are reasons to believe that a baptism of the Holy Spirit occurs at the point of our regeneration. Paul said to the Corinthians, "For by one Spirit we were all baptized into one bodywhether Jews or Greeks, whether slaves or freeand have all been made to drink into one Spirit" (1 Cor. 12:13). It is therefore not unscriptural to say that at our new birth we are baptized into or by the Holy Spirit. Spirit baptism is the life-transforming work of the regeneration of lost sinners. Every born-again believer enjoys the indwelling presence of the Holy Spirit.

6. On the other hand, there is strong scriptural evidence that there is a baptism of the Holy Spirit that takes place *after* our new birth. This has been the teaching both of the Holiness Movement and of the Pentecostalism that emerged from that movement. The conviction here is that though the Holy Spirit is with all believers, Holy Spirit baptism comes after the new birth, as a subsequent and distinct work of grace. Most here would agree that the baptism of the Holy Spirit involves at least the deeper cleansing of the heart. This is certainly the testimony of Pentecost, as seen in Acts 2 and 15. In 1 Thessalonians Paul also calls new believers to a deeper cleansing of their hearts (1 Thess. 4:7, 5:23). Many (though not all) Pentecostals believe that this Spirit baptism is accompanied by speaking in tongues.

7.  There are still others who say the baptism with the Holy Spirit is a third work of God's grace, subsequent to both the new birth and a second work of heart cleansing. The focus in this case is primarily on the receiving of greater power for service. What is clear is that the Holy Spirit continually motivates believers to purity of heart and power for service. That is why some also teach that there may be multiple baptisms with the Holy Spirit, while others say there is "one baptism but many fillings." Ephesians 5:18 points us in the direction of seeing a continual work of the Holy Spirit in our lives: "And do not be drunk with wine, in which is dissipation; but be filled with the Spirit." The progressive tense of the last verb is important, implying that we should continually "be being filled" with the Spirit.

8.  Finally, let us note that being filled with the Holy Spirit and living a Spirit-filled life means that we will walk in newness of life and that we will be conformed more and more into the image of Christ. In other words, we are not unholy people who are occasionally given miraculous gifts. We do not "operate in the Spirit" in the morning and then turn around and live like the devil in the afternoon. Rather, though the power of the Holy Spirit we are enabled to live the Christlike life day in and day out and thereby continually bring glory to our Father in heaven.

## Questions

1. What do you see as the difference between the Holy Spirit experience of Bezalel in the Old Testament and that of the 120 at Pentecost?

2. As taught in this lesson, what is the difference between the charismatic fullness of the Holy Spirit and the ethical fulness of the Holy Spirit?

3. Do believers receive the Holy Spirit into their hearts and lives when they are born again?

4. Explain at least two of the differing opinions about when the baptism with the Holy Spirit takes place in the life of believers.

5. What does it mean in practical terms to live a Spirit-filled life?

## Things to Think About

❖ *It is only through the power of the Holy Spirit that we are enabled to live the Christlike life.*

❖ *It is the privilege of every child of God to enjoy the daily cleansing power of the Holy Spirit.*

# THE MINISTRY OF THE HOLY SPIRIT IN THE CHURCH

### John 14:26; Acts 6:5,8; 7:55; 8:29; 13:2-4

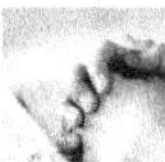

*But the Helper, the Holy Spirit, whom the Father will send in My name, He will teach you all things, and bring to your remembrance all things that I said to you. . . . they chose Stephen, a man full of faith and the Holy Spirit. . . . And Stephen, full of faith and power, did great wonders and signs among the people. . . . But he, being full of the Holy Spirit, gazed into heaven and saw the glory of God, and Jesus standing at the right hand of God, . . . Then the Spirit said to Philip, "Go near and overtake this chariot." . . . As they ministered to the Lord and fasted, the Holy Spirit said, "Now separate to Me Barnabas and Saul for the work to which I have called them." Then, having fasted and prayed, and laid hands on them, they sent them away. So, being sent out by the Holy Spirit, they went down to Seleucia, and from there they sailed to Cyprus.*

## Lesson Theme

When we look closely at the four gospels (Matthew, Mark, Luke, and John) and compare it with the Acts of the

Apostles, we see many contrasts, even though many of the principal actors or participants are the same. We see the apostles of Jesus (minus Judas Iscariot, of course) who are active in both the gospels and in Acts. However, one of the most striking differences is that while Jesus Christ, the Son of God, is the great center of focus in the gospels it is the Holy Spirit who emerges in the Acts of the Apostles as the great divine power at work. This is why some people suggest that the Acts of the Apostles could more properly be titled the Acts of the Holy Spirit. Beginning with the amazing outpouring of the Holy Spirit in Chapter 2, we can see the early disciples moving out here and there under the direction and power of the Holy Spirit. In this lesson we are looking at some of the details of the ministry of the Holy Spirit in the Early Church. It is ministry that is still going on even in our own day.

## Introduction

Prior to Jesus' departure from his disciples he gave them clear understanding about the important coming ministry of the Holy Spirit among them, especially as recorded in John 14 and 16. He let them know that the Holy Spirit would be with them forever. He said, "You know Him, for He dwells with you and will be in you" (John 14:16-17). He further explained that the Holy Spirit would "convict the world of sin, and of righteousness, and of judgment" (16:8). Further, Jesus said, "When He, the Spirit of truth, has come, He will guide you into all truth" (16:13). What Jesus was telling his disciples was that they would not be left on their own, but would be guided, protected and inspired by the ever-present help of the Holy Spirit. It would be their privilege to experience an empowerment and guidance unlike anything they had known while following Jesus. It is important for us to see clearly the reality of the ministry of the Holy Spirit in the Early Church, for it is that same reality that can and must be our own today.

## Lesson

1. One of the most important things we can see about the ministry of the Holy Spirit in the Early Church is what Jesus told them in John 14:26. He told them that the Holy Spirit would "teach them all things," and bring to their remembrance what Jesus had taught them while he was with them. The Holy Spirit was to be their teacher. One of the primary ways that has always happened has been through the divine inspiration of scripture, through the breath of the Holy Spirit. Paul noted that "All scripture is given by inspiration of God," and Peter explained further that "Prophecy never came by the will of man, but holy men of God spoke *as they were* moved <u>by the Holy Spirit</u>" (2 Peter 1:21). Jesus was telling his disciples that the Holy Spirit would be their guarantee of truth, their teaching, and their constant reminder of what Jesus had imparted to them during the course of his earthly ministry. Even today we can rely on the truth of the Bible because we know that through it the Holy Spirit has conveyed God's truth to us.

**The ministry of the Holy Spirit to the Church was one of the last promises Jesus gave to his disciples.**

2. We can see that quickly after Pentecost and the mighty infilling of the Holy Spirit it was through the power of the Holy Spirit that the apostles spoke the word of God. In Chapter 4, after Peter and John were arrested and then before the Sanhedrin, Luke says, "Then Peter, *filled with the Holy Spirit*, said to them, . . ." (Acts 8:8). Later, after they were released and returned to their brothers and sisters, we are told that "When they had prayed, the place where they were assembled together was shaken; and they were all *filled with the Holy Spirit*, and they spoke the word of God with boldness" (8:31). In this and many other ways we can see that the secret to the success of the Early Church was that they were filled with the Holy Spirit. They were moving in the power generated by the presence of the Holy Spirit.

3. There were multiple ways in which the presence and empowering of the Holy Spirit was evidenced in those early days. It was the Holy Spirit who moved them to

preach the word of God. When the angel of the Lord sent Philip toward Gaza and he encountered the Ethiopian eunuch, it was the Holy Spirit who told him, "Go near and overtake this chariot" (Acts 8:29). When they faced persecution and death it was the Holy Spirit who comforted them (Acts 9:31).

4.  The ministry of the early disciples was carried out under very specific leadership from the Holy Spirit. When the Church at Antioch experienced spiritual quickening and numerical growth it was the Holy Spirit who called out the first missionary team to head westward with the gospel. "As they ministered to the Lord and fasted, *the Holy Spirit said*, 'Now separate to Me Barnabas and Saul for the work to which I have called them.' Then, having fasted and prayed, and laid hands on them, they sent *them* away. So, *being sent out by the Holy Spirit*, they went down to Seleucia, . . ." (Acts 13:2-4). What we are seeing is that the Holy Spirit was directly involved in every step the early believers were taking.

5.  As Paul, Barnabas and other early Christians fanned out around the Mediterranean world the Holy Spirit continued to guide them, helping them at crucial points to make strategic decisions about where to go and where not to go. In Acts 16:6-7, for example, Luke tells us, "When they had gone through Phrygia and the region of Galatia, *they were forbidden by the Holy Spirit* to preach the word in Asia. After they had come to Mysia, they tried to go into Bithynia, but *the Spirit did not permit them*." What is remarkable here is that the early

Christians knew that it was the Holy Spirit who was guiding them. They heard the unmistakable voice and word of God, through the Person of the Holy Spirit, and they obeyed.

6.  It was through the empowering presence of the Holy Spirit that these early disciples were able to speak the word of God with boldness. They experienced signs and wonders not simply for their own amazement but to enable them to proclaim the saving word of God. "And when they had prayed, the place where they were assembled together was shaken; and they were all *filled with the Holy Spirit*, and they spoke the word of God with boldness" (Acts 4:31). The receiving of the fulness of the Holy Spirit resulted in clear and effective proclamation of the word of God, then further resulting in the salvation of multitudes.

7.  A practical question for all of us is how the Holy Spirit can and should be evidenced in our lives in our own day. Can we expect to see similar things in our own day? The truth is that we have all the privileges that were enjoyed by the Early Church. The power of the Holy Spirit has not diminished over the centuries. So, what can or should we expect today? First, just as with the early disciples we can rely on the sure guidance of the Holy Spirit. The Holy Spirit not only calls us to personal repentance and salvation, but he can guide us into the specific vocation or tasks God has for us to do. Paul told the Ephesians to "Walk worthy of the calling with which you were called" (Eph. 4:1).

8. The Holy Spirit will also empower us. That means he will give us the ability, strength and courage to do exactly what God has called us to do. Even Jesus himself walked "in the power of the Spirit" (Luke 4:14). He told the disciples they would receive power when the Holy Spirit came on them (Acts 1:8). It is very clear that they repeatedly experienced the empowering of the Spirit for the preaching of the gospel. We can and should experience that same power in our own day.

9. The Holy Spirit specifically empowers God's people for the purpose of evangelism. For example, Paul told the Thessalonians, "For our gospel did not come to you in word only, but also in power, and in the Holy Spirit" (1 Thess. 1:5). Peter also referred to "Those who have preached the gospel to you by the Holy Spirit sent from heaven" (1 Pet. 1:12). That same mighty Holy Spirit empowerment for evangelism is available to us today just as it was during New Testament times.

10. Finally, we know that it is through the Holy Spirit that we receive the spiritual gifts that are given for the common good of the Church (1 Cor. 12:7). There are many spiritual gifts mentioned in the scriptures (Rom. 12:3-8; 1 Cor. 12:1; 1 Peter 4:10-11), and there are no doubt others that are not specifically names. Each of those gifts is given as an important part of the ongoing ministry of the Holy Spirit in our own day. Surely Jesus was correct when he told his disciples that it was good for him to go away so the Holy Spirit could minister through the global Church. He is still at work today! Hallelujah.

## Questions

1. Why have some people suggested that the Acts of the Apostles could also be titled the Acts of the Holy Spirit?

2. What role did the Holy Spirit play in the writing of the scriptures?

3. Name some of the things that were accomplished in the Book of Acts through the ministry of the Holy Spirit.

4. What role did the Holy Spirit play in the launching of the first missionary journeys away from the city of Antioch?

5. What are some of the ways the Holy Spirit empowers his people in today's Church?

## Things to Think About

❖ *The Holy Spirit was active throughout the entire history of mankind, yet it is only in the Book of Acts that we see his ministry so constant and clear.*

❖ *Without the tarrying in Jerusalem for the outpouring of the Holy Spirit the Early Church would have fallen flat on their faces, never to rise again.*

# WORSHIPPING OUR GREAT GOD

### Psalm 96:7-9; Ephesians 5:18-20; 1 Timothy 1:17

*Give to the Lord, O families of the peoples, give to the Lord glory and strength. Give to the Lord the glory due His name; bring an offering, and come into His courts.  Oh, worship the Lord in the beauty of holiness! Tremble before Him, all the earth. . . . And do not be drunk with wine, in which is dissipation; but be filled with the Spirit, speaking to one another in psalms and hymns and spiritual songs, singing and making melody in your heart to the Lord, giving thanks always for all things to God the Father in the name of our Lord Jesus Christ, . . . Now to the King eternal, immortal, invisible, to God who alone is wise, be honor and glory forever and ever. Amen.*

## Lesson Theme

We cannot end our studies about our great and glorious God without underscoring the importance of worship. The ultimate purpose for human existence is to bring glory to God, and we do that most effectively through our worship. If our God were small, ineffective or unengaged in our lives and in our world, we could be excused for failing to worship him. But the truth is that we have a God who totally surpasses our understanding. His benefits to us are forever and without number or even comprehension. That is why we must talk in this lesson about our appropriate human response. We must re-dedicate ourselves to lives of wholesome and dedicated worship of God.

## Introduction

The word *worship* comes from the Old English word *weorpscipe*, meaning veneration or honor given to something. Its meaning is to ascribe "worthiness" or "worth-ship" to something. Therefore, our Christian worship is the act of giving reverence, honor, praise or homage to our great God. There are several words in the New Testament referring to worship, one of which is *proskuneo*, referring to bowing down before God or before an earthy king. In this lesson we will examine what worship is, how we can worship God for who he is, what he does and how he has benefited our own lives. We will also mention some of the scripturally-sound ways in which we can worship our God.

## Lesson

1.  The worship of our great God is a matter that can be both very private and also very public. Any form of worship that extols God in a reverent and sincere manner is valid worship and should be encouraged. It is impossible to imagine how any believer who has been

rescued from a life of sin and rebellion could refrain from giving praise to God, in one form or the other. It is a natural expression of our spirits as we consider who God is and what he has done for us and for others around us. In other words, worship is a natural giving of praise, honor and respect to the Father, Son and Holy Spirit. Our worship can take a great multiplicity of forms: singing, playing instruments of music, quietly meditating and praying, kneeling down, standing up, shouting out praises to God, waving our hands heavenward, etc.

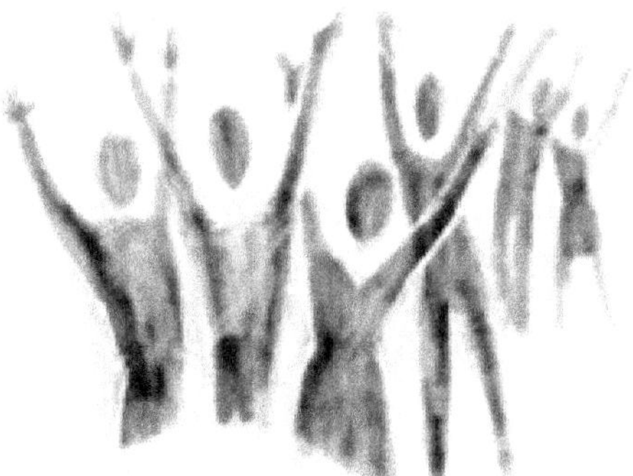

**There is nothing of greater eternal value and more lasting human benefit than humble worship to our great God.**

2. One of the most fundamental aspects of our worship of God is honoring him for who he is. As we have seen, worship is attributing "worth" to an object or a person. There is no being of higher worth in our universe than Almighty God. He is truly, as the philosopher Anselm said over 1,000 years ago, "that than which no greater can be conceived." He is of surpassing greatness. We

therefore worship him for his incomprehensible majesty, beauty, and splendor. Because the essence of God is love and holiness, we worship him and praise him for those qualities. We are never wasting our time when we worship God for who he is.

3. Worship also involves extoling and thanking God for what he does. We do not serve the God of the deists, who believe that God created the world and then left it to run on its own and who is now absent from the scene. God is actively engaged in his world and he deserves honor for all he does. Our God is a "very present help in trouble" (Ps. 46:1). Psalm 121:4 assures us that "He who keeps Israel shall neither slumber nor sleep." The huge difference between the God of African traditional religion and the God of the Bible is that he is present, active and constantly engaging with the human beings who are the keen object of his loving focus day and night. His purpose in our creation was precisely so he could fellowship with us, on the basis of shared character. He cries out to us, "You shall be holy, for I the Lord your God *am* holy" (Lev. 19:2; 1 Pet. 1:16) because he desires to walk with us in a personal relationship.

4. All of us can look around us in our world and see multiple ways in which God continues to sustain his creation. As modern astronauts have reached the moon, and are now aiming for Mars, and as astronomers are peering at distant stars and even planets in other solar systems, our wonder increases. We see that God's care for this planet Earth, and the sustaining of all of its

teaming life, is something for which much praise is due. Isaiah asks, "Who has measured the waters in the hollow of His hand, measured heaven with a span and calculated the dust of the earth in a measure? Weighed the mountains in scales and the hills in a balance?" (Isaiah 40:12). Truly we serve a great God who is eminently worthy of our worship.

5. Worshiping God also means that I extol him for what he has down in my own life. He has sustained me physically. He saw me safely through months of life in the womb, and then brought me out in safety. He has kept me alive throughout my years and has blessed me in uncountable ways. God spoke through Isaiah and said, "Fear not, for I *am* with you; be not dismayed, for I *am* your God. I will strengthen you, yes, I will help you, I will uphold you with My righteous right hand" (Is. 41:10).

6. Much more than that, however, my worship to God is because of what he has done in saving my soul, in rescuing me from the deceptions and slavery of sin and keeping me from the evil intentions of Satan even now. Paul told Timothy that "The Lord is faithful, who will establish you and guard *you* from the evil one" (2 Thess. 3:3). And centuries before that the psalmist David declared, in the all-time favorite psalm, "The Lord is my shepherd; I shall not want. . . . He restores my soul; . . . Yea, though I walk through the valley of the shadow of death, I will fear no evil; for You *are* with me; . . . Surely goodness and mercy shall follow me all the days

of my life; and I will dwell in the house of the Lord forever" (Ps. 23). Hallelujah!

7.  What are some of the scriptural ways in which we can worship our great God? One of the ancient symbols of worship is going down on our knees, or even sometimes prostrating ourselves entirely on our faces. "Oh come, let us worship and bow down; let us kneel before the Lord our Maker" (Ps. 95:6). In many cultures around the world such prostration is reserved for royalty or for those to whom we desire to show ultimate respect. Surely God deserves such respect more than any other.

8.  We can also demonstrate our worship by shouting, clapping our hands or singing praises. All of these means are clearly in evidence in the Bible and also in the worship of God's children throughout the ages. The Book of Psalms is the central Praise Book or Worship Book of the Bible, and in it we see all of these demonstrations. "Oh, clap your hands, all you peoples! Shout to God with the voice of triumph! . . . Sing praises to God, sing praises!" (Ps. 47:1,6).

9.  Raising or extending our hands in worship, as well as using all kinds of musical instruments, is also scripturally sounds. The raising of our hands is a sign both of holy recognition or who God is and of surrender. The use of instruments enhances our praise. The Book of Psalms ends with this powerful exhortation: "Praise Him with the sound of the trumpet; praise Him with the lute and harp! Praise Him

with the timbrel and dance; praise Him with stringed instruments and flutes! Praise Him with loud cymbals; praise Him with clashing cymbals! Let everything that has breath praise the Lord. Praise the Lord!" (Ps. 150:3-6)

## Questions

1. Explain the origins and meaning of the English word *worship*.

2. What are some of the things about the character of God that make him worthy of our praise?

3. Why are Bible believers more able to worship God than the deists or the African traditional religionists?

4. What are some of the ways of worshiping God that are mentioned in the scriptures?

5. What can you do in coming days, weeks and years to more effectively improve your worship habits?

## Things to Think About

❖ *The most satisfying and highest worship of God can only arise from the heart of a redeemed child of God. Other worship may exist, but it is far inferior.*

❖ *Let us live our lives so that they constitute continual praise to a never-failing God.*